Different Ways *of* Being an Educator

RELATIONAL PRACTICE

Ann Morgan, Ph.D.

BALBOA.
PRESS
A DIVISION OF HAY HOUSE

Balboa Press books may be ordered through booksellers or by contacting:

Balboa Press
A Division of Hay House
1663 Liberty Drive
Bloomington, IN 47403
www.balboapress.com.au
1 (877) 407-4847

Because of the dynamic nature of the Internet, any web addresses or links contained in this book may have changed since publication and may no longer be valid. The views expressed in this work are solely those of the author and do not necessarily reflect the views of the publisher, and the publisher hereby disclaims any responsibility for them.

The author of this book does not dispense medical advice or prescribe the use of any technique as a form of treatment for physical, emotional, or medical problems without the advice of a physician, either directly or indirectly. The intent of the author is only to offer information of a general nature to help you in your quest for emotional and spiritual well-being. In the event you use any of the information in this book for yourself, which is your constitutional right, the author and the publisher assume no responsibility for your actions.

Any people depicted in stock imagery provided by Thinkstock are models, and such images are being used for illustrative purposes only.
Certain stock imagery © Thinkstock.

Print information available on the last page.

ISBN: 978-1-5043-1205-9 (sc)
ISBN: 978-1-5043-1206-6 (e)

Balboa Press rev. date: 02/06/2018

Contents

*This book is dedicated to all educators who have walked alongside
young people as they re-engage in flexible learning programs
across Australia and in many parts of the world.*

*Your commitment, openness and generosity in sharing
your understanding of relational practice made this project possible.
You creatively navigate being an educator,
and co-learner with young people and colleagues.*

I am deeply grateful for who you are and what you do.

Ann Morgan, 2018

Think, feel and follow relationships.
Relationships are at the heart of social change.

Relationships require that we understand how and where things
connect and how this web of connections occupies the social
space where processes of change are birthed and hope to live.

John Paul Lederach (2005).

in their work with young people and colleagues. Questions were posed about what staff valued in their work – both personally and within the organisation. Other questions explored ways of professional learning and new staff induction. Throughout these books, research findings from educators are presented in three overarching themes that highlight different ways of being an educator in flexi schools. The three themes are the titles of the books.

A Series for Educators

Young people's perceptions and experience in alternative education settings in Australia and beyond have been well documented by researchers (see Appendices A and B). Other relevant topics within the broader field of alternative education are also documented in research (see Appendices A and B). Limited research on educator identity and development has been conducted in the context of alternative education or flexible learning choices programs, either nationally or internationally (Morgan, Brown, Pendergast, & Heck, 2013). For this reason, the research presented throughout this book contributes towards understanding educator identity and development in practice in a particular network of flexi schools. Educator identity is influenced by the context of these schools. Strengthening relationships is the first priority of practice in flexi schools. It cannot be overstated how important the young people themselves are in creating the unique culture of learning within flexi schools.

Ways of Working and Ways of Professional Learning

One of my passions and work responsibilities is to support educators as they make sense and meaning of their work in highly complex and innovative education settings that offer flexible learning pathways for young people who have been excluded (formally or informally) from traditional education settings. This has been my work over the last ten years. My hope is that by sharing the research findings in an accessible format, practitioners will be affirmed. Practical insights and strategies for understanding the broader questions around ways of working and ways of professional learning — "what are we doing", "why are we doing it" and "how do we do it better" — underlie the stories from practice that are included.

The books are designed to support practitioners as they engage in critical reflection. Questions exploring key aspects of practice are offered throughout the books as prompts for reflection. These books are a resource that can be used by individuals and within staff teams. They do not have to be read from cover to cover but can be accessed randomly or sequentially, depending on the specific needs of practitioners and the time available.

Personal and Professional Learning and Development

Educators in relationship with young people and colleagues navigate pathways of learning and development. The purpose of this learning and development is twofold. First, to refine practice in order to meet the learning needs of young people in relevant and meaningful ways. Second, a complementary priority is for educators to build their personal and professional capacity to sustain themselves in their practice – nurturing self-awareness and self-care.

The underlying philosophy and values that have shaped practice in flexi schools are outlined through the experiences and stories of educators. Operation by principles and the idea of common ground, that continue to inform life in these learning communities, are explored in these pages. Rather than following a set of rules, the four principles of respect, participation, safe and legal, and honesty, are used to guide all relationships. Adults and young people consider the four principles as they work towards finding common ground. This requires negotiating solutions to challenges that emerge within the learning community. Deeper insights into various aspects of practice, including the operation by principles model, are presented.

Ann Morgan, Ph.D.

Strategies and Resources for Relational Practice

For both those who are new to and those who wish to recover some of the passion for this work with young people, this book contains a series of questions for critical reflection. It also offers strategies for personal formation and growth that other practitioners have found informative and enriching. Challenges to dominant and outmoded education paradigms that no longer meet the needs of 21st Century learners are presented in accessible ways. For those willing to take a risk and become more alive in their own journey of being and becoming educators who are co-learners with young people and colleagues, this book offers some pathways and metaphoric maps to explore.

Acknowledgements

I wish to acknowledge my family, immediate and extended, connected by birth and informally adopted. I am who I am because of you. I know what I know through you. I share what I can because of your support. Deep thanks.

To my research supervisors, mentors and lifelong educators, too many to name, I thank you. To my professional colleagues — past and present — I thank and acknowledge you. The research was only possible in relationship with others.

To the young people we walk beside — past, present and future — I thank you and honour you. Your resilience and strength in the face of diversity is inspiring. You have taught and challenged me and I am grateful to be a co-learner with you alongside the educators you regularly engage with.

While this book has emerged from research and practice in flexi schools, I believe that the principles and values that underpin relational practice have relevance for educators in many contexts. My experience over 35 years in multiple education settings, including mainstream, international, and flexi school contexts, tells me this is so.

Introduction

The Story Behind the Work

The Centre Education Programme was initiated in 1986 when a small group of Christian Brothers, alongside a number of women from the Presentation Sisters, were seeking other ways of developing community and re-engaging young people in education in Logan City. At that time in the 1980s, Logan City was a rapidly growing, under-resourced urban region south of Brisbane. The Brothers collaborated with youth workers, social workers, local community members and teachers. They began to consider different ways of being in relationship with young people that challenged traditional hierarchical notions of schooling. The operation by principles model incorporating respect, participation, safe and legal, and honesty was adopted from youth workers and social workers who were working at that time in the youth sector (Youth Sector Training Manual, 1990). This model required adults to position themselves in more democratic, mutual and supportive relationships with young people and their families or carers.

This way of working requires another set of skills and different dispositions from those adopted by many educators in conventional schools (see Appendix C). It requires a shift towards a new paradigm of education that aligns with Catholic social teaching and the work of Edmund Rice, the Irish founder of the Christian Brothers who started a school for young boys living in poverty in Ireland in the early 19th Century. In Logan City, almost 200 years later, the Christian Brothers, like their founder Edmund Rice, wanted to improve the economic and social opportunities for young people in their local context. This model of education focuses on the dignity of every individual, balanced with the importance of the common good of the learning community.

Advocates of the model make a choice to stand in solidarity with those who are disenfranchised and marginalised. It requires a willingness from educators to develop authentic and respectful relationships with young people and their families and carers.

In hindsight it has become clear that this educational model aligns and connects with the aspirations and visions of other innovative educators. Agents of social change such as Dewey (democratic education), Freire (liberation through dialogue and the empowerment of voice), Rogers (unconditional positive regard), Illich (deschooling), and Vygotsky (sociocultural perspectives) come to mind. These thinkers and innovators developed philosophies, theories and practices that challenged dominant models of education in their time and context.

The model of education discussed in this book has emerged and developed through a shared vision, shared practice and the willingness of many committed practitioners to learn by doing, through trial and error, to create inclusive learning communities. This model speaks back to an education system that is failing to accommodate the diversity of students' life circumstances and learning needs. Identifying young people as the source of the problem of low school completion (te Riele, 2007) indicates the failure of conventional school systems to at least acknowledge, or at best address the needs of marginalised young people. This problem is recognised as a limitation of a system struggling to renew and update to more contemporary pedagogies that are student-centred and responsive to the changing needs of young people in contemporary society (Foundation for Young Australians (FYA), 2017; Kalantzis & Cope, 2005; Miller, 2005; Smyth, 2003; Whitby, 2013; Wyn, 2008).

My Personal Experience of this Model of Education

In 1992 I lived and worked in Logan City with the Christian Brothers. Through the programs they offered I became aware of a unique group of learners that required an innovative, creative and flexible approach to re-engagement and learning — an example of which was being prototyped at the Centre Education Programme. "Centre Ed" as it was known in the local community, was an educational experiment that prioritised relational learning. Over time it was registered as a school. Young people who were labelled as "chronic truants" in other contexts, were regular attendees. Many of these young people had been formally expelled or suspended from mainstream contexts due to a variety of challenging life circumstances.

Sixteen years later in 2008, after travelling, having a family, working in a community organisation, further teaching, and learning about leadership through practice in mainstream education contexts, I returned to working with staff in flexi schools. This network of flexi schools has experienced a rapid period of growth and expansion under the umbrella of Edmund Rice Education Australia (EREA), Youth+. My work involves staff support, professional learning and formation in the ethos and social justice values of the organisation, including the early vision of the Christian Brothers who established their first flexi school in Logan City.

A commitment to research within the organisation provided an opening to apply for a PhD scholarship associated with an Australian Research Council Industry Partnership between EREA and Griffith University. Alongside my part-time role in flexi schools, I engaged in fulltime doctoral studies exploring educator identity and development in the context of flexi schools – a privileged opportunity for which I am extremely grateful.

My Current Practice with Educators in Flexi Schools

Since the beginning of 2013, after completing my studies, I have been working in EREA Youth+ on a fulltime basis. My work has again focussed on staff support, professional learning and formation within the staff teams across a network of flexi schools in south-east Queensland. The work of educators in these settings is extremely rewarding, complex and, at times, demanding. There are many practical skills needed to re-engage young people and to support their wellbeing as they attend flexi schools. For staff, the importance of personal development, self-care and critical reflection is essential. These skills complement a wide range of other professional learning that educators commit to as part of their work with young people.

PART I

Ways of Working with Young People

1

Working in and through Relationships

Educators who work in flexi schools address the particular needs and interests of young people who choose to re-engage in flexible learning pathways. In the process of walking alongside young people, educators in flexi schools are provided with many opportunities for critical reflection to develop greater self-awareness and awareness of others. Engaging in education for transformation offers encounters with complexity that challenge and change perspectives on the nature and purpose of education, the nature and purpose of what it means to be a learner, and traditional notions of what it means to be an educator.

In flexi schools, the term *educator* is used in its broadest sense to include all adults in the learning community who enter into authentic, respectful relationships with young people. Teachers, youth workers, social workers, counsellors, music, arts and outdoor education workers, administrators, support and kitchen staff, artisans, technicians, crafts people, grounds people, and community volunteers all have an educative role as they engage in relational learning with young people. In this book I will generally use the term *educator(s), staff* and *colleague(s)* interchangeably. Where appropriate, for discussion around particular themes of practice, for example multidisciplinary practice, specific reference to different roles such as youth workers, social workers, community service workers or teachers, will be made. Through relational practice, educators' professional identities are influenced and changed through engagement with young people and colleagues. This occurs in ways that are often different from educators' experiences in conventional education contexts.

2

The *Relational Shift* in Working with Young People

In recent years, general trends in education towards more student-centred notions of teaching, with more emphasis on learning rather than teaching, are apparent (Beijaard, 1995). Within the network of flexi schools, this overt emphasis on young, person-centred, relational practice requires, in the first instance, that educators build relationships of trust and safety. These relationships support young people in moving from "isolation to connection" (Downey, 2009), following experiences of trauma, neglect, and abuse that are common for many young people in the context (Morgan, Pendergast, Brown, & Heck, 2015). Understanding the complex needs of this group of young people requires a process of awareness raising and professional learning for educators with a teaching background. Shifts in understanding are necessary for educators to be able to engage with young people in a safe and supportive manner to reduce "relational distance" (Vadeboncoeur, 2011) and redress "relational poverty" to increase well-being (Perry, 2009).

Moving from Task Orientation towards Greater People Orientation

In all aspects of practice in flexi schools, relationships are prioritised (Morgan, 2013; Morgan et al., 2015). Insights have been gained into the kinds of shifts and movements that educators make as they explore new and different ways of being educators and as they negotiate and co-construct who they are as educators in relationship with young people and with colleagues. A key difference in the relational work in the flexi schools' context and that of conventional schools is that most of the young people in flexi schools have been formally or informally excluded from conventional school contexts. Many young people in flexi schools have faced, and continue to face, multiple complexities that are often not acknowledged or addressed constructively in conventional school contexts. Subsequently, young people have resisted and rebelled against aspects of conventional schooling that have been detrimental to their identities and sense of well-being.

The reasons for the inability of school systems to respond proactively to the needs of young people are also complex. Time and sufficient resources are not always allocated to those who don't fit conventional schooling. Blaming individual young people or teachers in general is not helpful. Possible solutions lie in looking at the situation differently, considering how to change educational provision (te Riele, 2007). Rather than demanding compliance from young people whose life circumstances create barriers to learning, more creative, strengths-based, and solution-focused thinking and processes are required.

Against the Grain: Social and Political Agendas Impacting Educational Provision

Unfortunately, in the current social and political climate in Australia and internationally, punitive and overly simplistic solutions are increasingly being adopted in reaction to young people who have diverse needs and don't fit conventional schools. This group of young people require multifaceted and proactive responses due to external circumstances that influence their educational outcomes. There are systemic limitations that have contributed to young people's marginalisation and social exclusion (Morgan et al., 2014). In Australia, the link between low socio-economic status, disadvantage, or being Indigenous, or living in remote geographic locations has been identified in the Melbourne Declaration as contributing to inequitable educational outcomes (MCEETYA, 2008). One way to challenge education provision is to work with educators to interrogate their own values, beliefs, and assumptions about the nature of education, the nature of learning and learners, and what it means to be an educator.

Ann Morgan, Ph.D.

The Relational Shift

Educator identity in flexi schools is developed over time; learning occurs through practice and through critical reflection on practice. I refer to this learning process as the *relational shift* that captures four movements educators make in terms of their sense of identity as educators (see figure 1).

1. A Shift towards "Relationships First"

Relationships are the starting point for re-engaging young people and for developing supportive staff teams. Authentic relationships with young people and colleagues are characterised by certain dispositions of educators. For example, in interviews, educators talked about being fully human, being open, and being respectful. Educating the whole person is a priority.

Safe and supportive relationships are developed through informal education and working outside the boundaries of traditional classrooms. Genuinely listening to young people to focus on their individual learning needs supports the development of learning choices that are young-person centred.

Using the four principles influences the way educators are prepared to resolve conflict, acknowledge the challenges of the work, remain flexible, and let go of the need to know all and do all. These shifts towards collaboration and cooperation are influenced by the importance of relationships in the flexi schools' context between young people and staff colleagues. Becoming an educator and a learner through working in teams requires time and a gradual attainment of expertise in collaboration with more-experienced others. Through relationships with more experienced staff, educators are able to shift towards developing a deeper understanding of the complex needs of this group of young people.

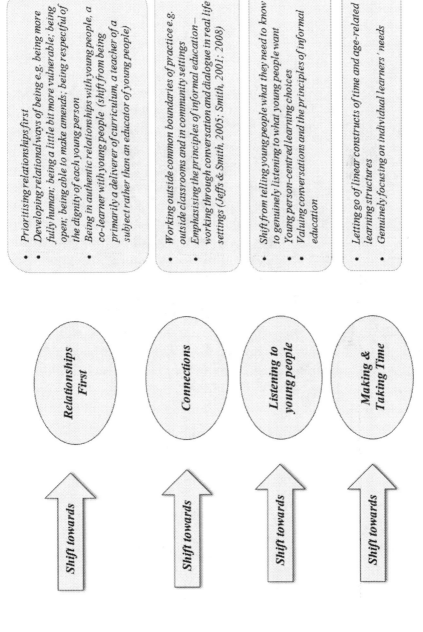

Figure 1. The Relational Shift in working with young people – Moving from task orientation to greater people orientation.

2. A Shift Towards Making "Connections"

Educators support young people to make connections for well-being and to reduce the risk of isolation (both within the school community and in the wider community). This influences educators' sense of identity and development in practice. For teachers, this shift requires working outside some of the common boundaries of practice experienced in conventional school settings (e.g., outside traditional classroom settings). For youth workers, social workers, and other workers from community services backgrounds, this emphasis on relationships sometimes provides an opportunity for validation of the ways of working that are common in their professional practice.

Drawing on principles from informal education, in which learning takes place in real-life settings, through relationships, and in conversation (Smith, 2008), working relationally is often more familiar for educators from community services backgrounds. Working in community settings and supporting young people to make relational connections within and beyond the school are also familiar aspects of practice for these educators. Another recognisable element of practice for some educators is making connections to life, to lifelong learning and to the wider community. In this sense, wider community might include parents or carers, and cultural groups. For other educators, this aspect of practice in the community context requires them to move beyond their own professional boundaries that influence their sense of educator identity and development in practice.

3. A Shift Towards "Listening to Young People"

As educators become more comfortable with prioritising relationships, and are able to recognise the significance of emphasising relationships with young people as the starting point of their work, they seem to become able to listen more effectively to young people. Listening is seen as a practical strategy to understand the needs of young people. Listening to understand involves appreciating what young people need, what they want, what they are interested in and what they are passionate about.

When educators are actively listening to young people they more often experience greater freedom to implement re-engagement strategies and provide more relevant and meaningful learning options for young people. Active listening can be defined as the capacity to listen sensitively to another (Rogers & Farson, 1957), showing "responsivity and empathy" (Hutchby, 2005, p. 304). Active listening seems to enable adults to let go of time frames for learning that are frequently attached to specific age groupings in conventional school settings. This letting go of imposed structures of conventional education systems means that educators can be more responsive to the individual young person's needs, rather than caught in the social and system expectations of learning and development that are frequently content driven or age-related (Fielding & Moss, 2011). Reform agendas that are inflexible, do not necessarily meet the complex changing needs of young people in the 21st Century (Dwyer & Wyn, 2001; Smyth et al., 2004; Wyn, 2008) and should not drive how young people are educated.

4. A Shift Towards "Making Time and Taking Time"

Being attuned to young people's developmental needs, encompassing physical, spiritual, emotional, social and intellectual dimensions, requires a shift in educator identity and development in practice. Teacher-trained educators have to let go of tendencies to impose linear constructs of time that require educational outcomes to be aligned with specific age levels, or associated with curriculum content. Inflexible reform agendas that do not acknowledge the need for integrated support services to address "multiple barriers (individual, family and structural) that prevent social and economic participation for many Australians" (Horn, 2010, p. 1) are also problematic. The shift towards making time and taking time requires educators to focus on learners' needs to avoid further marginalisation and social exclusion.

The Struggle to Change Default Patterns in Educator Identity

At times these shifts in educator identity and development are sites of personal and professional struggle. Tensions are evident for some teachers who are concerned about not being a *"proper teacher"* if they are not able to see and deliver "legitimate" curriculum and "measurable"

These assumptions, values and beliefs are influenced and shaped by our worldview and our socioeconomic and cultural positioning. The purpose of critical reflection is to bring to our awareness those points of struggle — those challenging places in which we find ourselves "stuck". Possibilities for transformation and liberation in our thinking and actions in practice will hopefully assist us to be more effective in our work with young people. This perspective has implications for how challenging issues in practice can be addressed constructively.

Understanding the Needs of Young People

The first category in ways of working with young people identified in interviews with staff was *understanding the needs of young people*. Figure 3 shows the common threads within this first category.

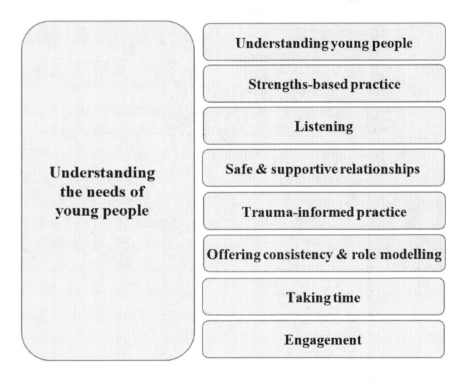

Figure 3. Common threads in understanding the needs of young people.

Understanding Young People

Understanding the needs of young people incorporated educators talking about *understanding young people*. Educator comments included: *"understanding the kids – not writing them off" (INT 11); "understanding where they are at" (INT 2)*; and *"starting where they are at" (INT 4)*.

Critical reflection for self-awareness and awareness of others:

Being understood

- *What attracted you to work with young people in flexi schools?*
- *How do you learn about the needs of young people?*
- *Have you ever experienced a relationship with an educator who was really focussed on your needs?*
- *Spend 5 minutes journaling or talking with a colleague about your experiences of having your learning needs understood.*

Strengths-Based Practice

The notion of understanding young people was further nuanced by a number of educators when they described how they adopted a strengths perspective to young people rather than a deficit approach, which requires seeing the dignity and potential of the young people rather than only noticing their problems (McCashen, 2005). This perspective is captured in the following response:

> *If you can somehow break those barriers down and get to know that person. There's a rich little person in there, that's got a lot of really cool opinions . . . everyone's got something really great to do or give or learn. (INT 14)*

A strengths-based approach to working with young people was articulated by another educator when she said:

> *Many of these young people have always been regarded by really good professionals as, you know, having deficits ... So there's no wonder that that young person after a number of years come to the conclusion that 'Oh I'm the problem and I carry these things with me that are the problem'. So if you don't work from that model, if you start with another model of "look at your strengths". (INT 10)*

Critical reflection for self-awareness and awareness of others:

Seeing potential and strengths

- *Can you identify and list your own strengths?*
- *What difference did it make to you when someone acknowledged your strengths and had confidence in your ability?*
- *Have you experienced a relationship with a significant person in your life (e.g., parent, teacher, boss, significant other) who seemed to focus on your weaknesses or limitations? How did this affect you?*
- *How might these experiences influence your practice with young people? (Consider underlying assumptions, values, and beliefs.)*

Ann Morgan, Ph.D.

Listening

Listening has been seen by educators as a practical strategy to understand the needs of young people. One of the teachers had a strong sense of the need to listen to young people in order to understand them and to be directed in action by their expressed needs. *"I think that's the essence of it, if we keep as adults getting back to listening to young people and what they're looking for" (INT 16)*. The commitment to listen to young people was driven by another participant's confidence in young people's resilience and capacity to cope:

> Um, it's listening, listening, listening and then trying to act upon what you hear with the understanding that often what young people say is not often what they mean and trying to keep talking and listening so that you can find out what they mean . . . not to fix the issue or their problem, but to help give them ways to look at it and cope with it. (INT 10)

Critical reflection for self-awareness and awareness of others:

Listening and being heard

- *Who has been an active listener in your life?*
- *What does it feel like to be heard?*
- *Did being heard change or influence your self-esteem or ability to participate in life and learning? In what ways?*
- *How do you show others you are actively listening?*
- *Do you seek feedback from others about your capacity to listen and be present with young people and colleagues?*

Safe and Supportive Relationships

Educators also spoke of understanding young people in terms of the need to develop *safe and supportive relationships* which offer a sense of connection and belonging (Thayer-Bacon, 2004). The priority of relationships was highlighted by an educator who said that, *"Staff really need to be aware that the curriculum is second and the relationships are first. [New teaching staff] come in with it the other way round" (INT 12)*.

For another educator the establishment of safe and supportive relationships with young people and taking the opportunity to really know the young people made a big difference to her work, especially with some young people whose behaviour she described as particularly challenging. *"You know what makes them tick and how they work and what's happening, it's a totally different experience"* (INT 09). In terms of safe and supportive relationships, the need for commitment from staff to young people was also mentioned as important: *"I think in order to create a bit of stability in these young people's lives you need people that are committed to stay longer" (INT 08)*.

Critical reflection for self-awareness and awareness of others:

Sources of safety and support

- *Who are the people that offer you support in your role?*
- *What difference have safe and supportive relationships made in your work life? Can you give practical examples?*
- *In what situations have you felt a lack of safety and support in relationships? How did this affect you?*
- *What actions have you taken to remedy these situations of feeling unsafe or unsupported?*
- *How do you encourage young people to do this in their relationships at school, at home, and at work?*

Engagement

In relation to understanding the learning needs of young people and strategies for *engagement*, some staff discussed the importance of offering practical, hands-on approaches with real-life connections (Margonis, 2004). One teacher mentioned that she tried to connect all her curriculum work to real life issues – this was her way of understanding the needs of young people for relevance and meaning, by starting with their own experience.

> *I think doing all sorts of life connections helps and that is not necessarily totally only life skills but when you're doing science you make the connection to life and sometimes you make the connection of really big philosophical questions to life – like you don't just focus on how to fill in a form, there has to be other stuff as well. (INT 04)*

Connecting to the interests of young people in a range of contexts outside of the classroom was an engagement strategy described by another educator.

> *A good example would be Maths, so that you don't have to have a Maths class, . . . Maths can be taught in the woodwork class, it can be taught out when you're out playing volleyball or basketball. It can be taught on the beach, so, trying to look at the curriculum areas in a completely different way. (INT 12)*

Critical reflection for self-awareness and awareness of others:

Engagement: Finding your passion

- *What are you passionate about? What really energizes you?*
- *When was the last time you pursued an activity you are passionate about? How did it influence your wellbeing?*
- *Who has supported you in finding and pursuing your passion?*
- *Have you ever been in a situation where you were coerced or forced to do something or learn about something was of no interest to you?*
- *How did you react in the situation?*
- *What has motivated you to remain engaged in something when you were struggling to do so?*

Recognising the Agency of Young People

The second category identified in interview data analysis was *recognising the agency of young people* (see figure 2, p.?). Agency refers to young people's capacity to act on the world. Staff talked about how they recognised young people's agency in a variety of ways. Figure 4 shows the common threads under this category.

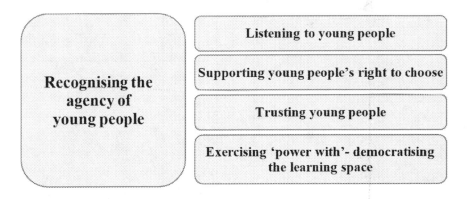

Figure 4. Common threads in recognising the agency of young people.

Within each category a series of common threads are presented. Questions that prompt critical reflection are included. You are invited to use these questions to assist individual reflection or to support discussions with supervisors, mentors and staff teams. Flexibility is built in — the choice is yours! Remember, critical reflection can occur in a variety of ways and in a range of settings.

Ann Morgan, Ph.D.

Listening to Young People

Listening to young people was a common thread related to recognising the agency of young people. Listening to young people included the need to be informed by the young people and the importance of acting on what is heard from the young people. This was summed up by an educator when she said: *"Before I can do anything, I need to be informed by the young people, and then it's a matter of making that connection"* (INT 01). According to staff, listening supports young people to enact their own solutions, allowing them to drive outcomes according to what they themselves are looking for. An educator recognised that young people can work out their own solutions and that they mainly want to be heard.

> *You don't always want to give them the solutions, 'cause they have it. They have it, they know it. It's about you helping them get to their solution, and actually making them think about it ... they just don't want you to tell them, they just want you to listen. (INT 13)*

Critical reflection for self-awareness and awareness of others:

Being an active listener

- *How do you actively listen to young people?*
- *Who gives you feedback on this aspect of your practice?*
- *Are you aware of certain circumstances and situations that block you from actively listening?*
- *Can you bring your awareness of your own assumptions, values, beliefs, and past experiences that may contribute to certain blocks that you experience?*

Supporting Young People's Right to Choose

Another common thread in recognising the agency of young people was *supporting young people's right to choose.* This was discussed in a number of ways including the need to respect the choices made by young people even in the face of disagreement. This notion was linked to a rights perspective, highlighting the young people's right to choose and not trying to force young people to do what adults perceive they should.

> *I think I've built up a really good detachment from the young people, even though I love them dearly, and I want the best for them, but they've still got to make their choices and they've got to live their lives . . . I s'pose it's always remembering to respect the young person, it's their right to choose, positive or negative it's their right to choose and that's the hard bit cause you want to wrap them up. (INT 02)*

Working with young people as they find their own passion was perceived by another educator as an important dimension of young people's agency.

> *I really enjoy the kind of adult, young adult to adult kind of model. You're here "cause you want to be" . . . not kind of trying to force people to do things . . . Just helping people find their passion. Once they've got a passion . . . you do support and stuff, but when they've got a passion then they've got a drive, they've got a reason to do stuff. (INT 03)*

Critical reflection for self-awareness and awareness of others:

Having choices

- *Have you experienced having limited choices in something that affected your own life? What actions did you take?*
- *Are you aware of times when you have tried to impose your will/ perspective on others, including young people?*
- *What reactions did you get?*

- *What could you do differently to ensure that young people are making choices and taking responsibility for their choices?*
- *In making choices, how do you balance individual needs with the common good of the learning community? How do you deal with compromise and contradictions?*

Trusting Young People

Respecting the capacity of young people to make choices can be linked to *trusting young people*. Trust was expressed in three ways: trusting what young people want; trusting what young people know; and trusting what young people can do. What young people want was linked to them finding their own "spark" and "passion". *"I guess people doing things that they want to. People getting spark, people getting passion - I value that" (INT 03).*

Trusting what young people know was captured by a teacher who fostered young people's agency by trusting that they already had a significant knowledge and a skill base. She was conscious of highlighting this as she supported young people who were choosing to re-engage in education.

> *. . . but it's sort of letting them understand how they've actually already got a whole lot of skills, but perhaps not the awareness around those skills, and that's the basis of their learning, they've actually learnt a whole lot. (INT 01)*

Trusting what young people can do requires educators to share responsibility with young people. This was seen in situations requiring planning and organising:

> *. . . just organising outings, and stuff like that. It's only an hour but, like this term we might organise a half day thing, or a full day thing or a camp. But you know, go play basketball, go for a walk down the beach, we'll go and do that, stuff like that. It's up to them to organise it. (INT 11)*

It was also evident in situations requiring problem solving of issues:

> *And at the end of the day . . . which is what I do with the grade 11s and other young people today is to say, it's up to you, you know it's our school, it's not my school, it's your school. Like you need to bring your responsibility, you need to bring your participation and respect. (INT 10)*

Another example of staff trusting what young people can do with their peers was seen in a story about a group of young people supporting each other outside the school.

> *One young person was ready to take off. And yet, two or three others, in particular one other, but there were two or three standing in the background beckoning that other person back. Just saying, you know, 'this can be worked out'. And I think that that's part of it. Jay is wanting to walk out the door and you've got three other young people saying no, don't do that. Come back and we can get it sorted. There is a better way'.*
> *(INT 07)*

Critical reflection for self-awareness and awareness of others:

The gift of trust

- *Are you trustworthy? Do you easily trust others?*
- *Who are the people who have placed their trust in you?*
- *How did being trusted affect you? How did it make you feel?*
- *Can you recall a situation when you felt let down by someone you trusted?*
- *Can you recall a situation when someone who trusted you felt that you let them down?*
- *How did you resolve these challenging situations?*

Exercising "Power With" — Democratising the Learning Space

Finally, recognising the agency of young people through listening, supporting choice, respecting their right to choose and trusting them, ultimately leads to a change in the power dynamics between adults and young people in the learning community – exercising 'power with' rather than 'power over' young people (Slattery, Butigan, Pelicaric, & Preston-Pile, 2005, p. 115; Starhawk, 1988; Warren, 2005). The common thread of exercising 'power with' requires adults to foster more mutual and collaborative relationships with young people (Nabavi & Lund, 2012), shifting the power dynamic inherent in more traditional teacher/student roles in which the teacher is situated as the expert and the young person as the recipient of teacher expertise. A number of educators talked about their perceptions of having as much to learn from young people as they have to teach young people. Vygotsky describes this quality of teaching and learning relationship through his concept of "obuchenie", which captures the idea that all participants are both teachers and learners, and every act of teaching is also an act of learning (Cole, 2009; Vadeboncoeur, 2011). This kind of mutuality requires a letting go of traditional paradigms of control in order to embrace and enact cooperative paradigms (Kalantzis & Cope, 2005).

The notion of a cooperative paradigm was expressed in the words of an educator with a social work background:

> *I guess I don't want to be seen as an authority person. I'm not above them, we're all people in this community and that's how I'm gonna approach it in a respectful way and not that I'm a senior person in this environment. I don't want to be seen or approached in that way.*
>
> *I feel I have as much to learn from the young people here as they have to learn from me. [There is] that real feeling that we're all on a level playing field. (INT 06)*

A degree of humility and the capacity to demonstrate one's humanity through sometimes being vulnerable was perceived by some staff as important. For example, being able to admit mistakes and apologise to other educators or young people, or being willing to show sensitivity through emotions, demonstrates shifts in power dynamics. One educator described it as openness to being vulnerable and sensitive to what the young people have to offer.

> *I think it happens by being open to the fact of, by being a little bit vulnerable. By putting yourself out there and doing the normal things and doing them sort of sensitively, you know where young people are coming from . . . having a sensitivity to young people and what they've got to offer as well. (INT 07)*

Critical reflection for self-awareness and awareness of others:

Power dynamics — are you aware?

- *What has informed your understanding of power dynamics?*
- *Have you ever felt disempowered?*
- *What was the situation?*
- *How did this affect you personally?*
- *Are you aware of the ways you exercise power with young people and colleagues?*
- *How do you judge or evaluate this? Do you regularly seek feedback on your use of power from young people and colleagues who have observed your practice?*

Learning Choices Support

The third category in staff perceptions of effective ways of working with young people was *learning choices support*. The following common threads were identified (see figure 5).

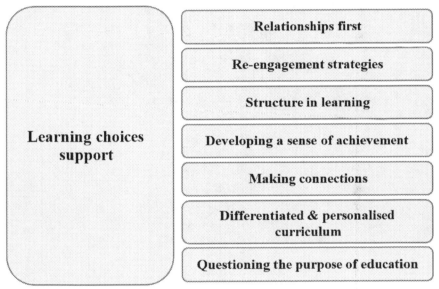

Figure 5. Common threads in learning choices support.

Within each category a series of common threads are presented. Questions that prompt critical reflection are included. You are invited to use these questions to assist individual reflection or to support discussions with supervisors, mentors and staff teams.

Relationships First

Common threads in the third category of learning choices also support an emphasis on *relationships first*. In their stories, educators highlighted that, for young people to learn, it was essential for educators to first develop positive relationships with them. The ability to relate to others was a positive educational outcome for young people that these educators spoke about:

> *I love that the relationships come first and, I mean as an educator we know that's the most important thing, that is somebody's comfortable and confident … that's what's going to provide them with opportunities in terms of relationships, friendships, social networking and work – and that's the most important thing you know. (INT 09)*

This shift to prioritising relationships first can sometimes be challenging for new staff.

> *[When new staff] become more relaxed they become more aware that the content of a curriculum isn't all that significantly important in the young people's life at the moment. It's not denying the value of learning but learning is, well you start by saying, education is much broader than two As, Bs or Cs. (INT 05)*

Critical reflection for self-awareness and awareness of others:

Relationships first

- *Who were the educators in your life who influenced you most positively and those who influenced you most negatively?*
- *How did their influence affect your learning?*
- *Can you define your understanding and philosophy about the nature and purpose of education?*
- *Where are the points of congruence and those of tension between your personal philosophy and what happens within your flexi school context?*
- *In what ways might your educational philosophy affect the learning of young people in your care?*

Re-engagement Strategies

The second common thread in learning choices support was identified as *re-engagement strategies*. Making real-life connections, and doing hands-on and practical activities were some re-engagement strategies identified by staff.

> *I find that the kids also respond really well to the feeling of having learned something ... and the internet helps and that's one thing that works with them is finding all sorts of curious demonstrations on the internet – all sorts of interactive things that they can manipulate.(INT 04)*

Another important strategy for re-engagement was making the young people the centre of learning. *"Just joining in is the first step under really structured guidelines ... and the kids are always the centre of my curriculum" (INT 14).*

Enjoyment in the learning process for staff and young people was also identified as a strategy for re-engaging young people. As one educator put it:

> *What I do is, if I have to teach something I make it enjoyable for myself. So I go how will I make it so it's enjoyable for myself to teach? And it will be enjoyable for the kids. So that's the way I approach it and it works. (INT 11)*

An educator articulated his view of what education should be:

> *For me personally I never really liked just sitting in a classroom and being fed information after information. For me, education shouldn't be that way; it should be interactive; it should be fun; it should be engaging. (INT 08)*

Critical reflection for self-awareness and awareness of others:

Re-engagement strategies

- *Think of a time when you have been totally engaged or immersed in learning something — what were the specific conditions that contributed to your level of engagement?*

- *How do you observe or check in with young people about their levels of engagement in learning?*
- *Are your own learning preferences similar or different to those of the young people in your learning group?*
- *How do you make use of these differences & similarities?*

Structure in Learning

The need for *structure in learning* was the third common thread in learning choices support identified in the stories of practitioners. Some staff perceived this was important given the complexities in other areas of the young people's lives. *"I think that the young people are often looking for structure too. Because, um, quite often we find that by the time that they've found us, a lot of structure in their life has gone" (INT 01).*

Structure can be provided to young people in the early stages of attendance at a program, and was evident in the scaffolding of activities to accommodate intermittent attendance. *"We've overlayed quite a lot of structure to support intermittent attendees" (INT 01).* The need for clarity from the teacher about learning goals and processes was seen as important. *"The other thing that works is structure and real [clarity] about what's happening when" (INT 04).*

Critical reflection for self-awareness and awareness of others:

Structure in learning

- *How do you provide structure and flexibility in your learning group at your flexi school?*
- *How attached are you to your own view of structure?*
- *How do you negotiate structure and routine in your learning environment?*
- *How do you ensure the structures and routine in your learning space do not become static or rigid?*
- *Do you discuss with young people the benefits and challenges of routines, rhythms and rituals in learning?*
- *How do you accommodate differences in your learning space while promoting a sense of community and belonging?*

A Sense of Achievement

Assisting young people to develop *a sense of achievement* was a common thread when educators discussed learning choices support for young people. A sense of achievement was gradually attained by young people when educators acknowledged what young people already knew and what they have learnt. It was recognised that young people liked to have the sense of achievement that accompanied successful learning.

> *Some of the greatest excitement that they've [young people] ever had was passing a Maths exam, whilst we say it's not that important it is really important to them because it's what society will label them as and they acknowledge that – it's only when they get a pass or when they get an A or a B, they actually are prepared to say that society has labelled me as an E and I'm not really an E. So it's all nice to deny that that's important but the young people do know that it's significant. (INT 05)*

Developing the aspirations and confidence of young people in their own ability to learn was considered essential for learning choices support. The need to strengthen young people's self-esteem and capacity to get along with other people was viewed as important in foregrounding learning. Strengthening relationships was viewed as a contributing factor towards better academic achievement for young people through developing self-confidence and self-trust.

> *I see success as engagement, no matter how small or big it is. Um, and success to me is the young people here having ownership of this place. You know Maths and English all that can come later … one of the boys, he got a C for [school subject] and he said "well, how do I get a B?" and I said "Well, trust yourself". So he did. I said, "Trust your judgement, trust yourself". Cause he was very hesitant. And, he did. And then he thanked me for it. That's it – self-belief with the kids. (INT 11)*

Critical reflection for self-awareness and awareness of others:

A sense of achievement

- *What has been your greatest personal achievement?*
- *How have you experienced failure?*
- *What was this experience like for you?*
- *What did you learn from it?*
- *How do you measure success and achievement for yourself?*
- *How do you measure success and achievement for young people?*
- *Where do the challenges lie for you in this area of practice?*

Making Connections

The importance of *making connections* was the fifth common thread in learning choices support. Connections with people, connections with their own interests and connecting young people to the things they need to know in terms of future transitions, were some of the ways staff discussed the idea of making connections. One educator saw herself as a kind of connector:

> *I guess I've often seen myself in lots of work as a kind of "connector" so that it's about connecting young people with other things that they need to know, like, having a really good idea of what's around and then doing some connecting with things that they need to do, as much as like having relationships here or wherever I was working, but I really thought that connecting people onwards after they've been here was a really good tool. (INT 03)*

Making connections to one's own life experience was also viewed by an educator as a way to engage young people in learning choices. "*I draw on my knowledge and life experience and the things that I think young people can do practically*" *(INT 12)*.

Critical reflection for self-awareness and awareness of others:

Making connections

- *What do you do to foster connections in the learning choices you negotiate with young people (within and beyond your flexi)?*
- *How do you encourage and support young people to draw on their lived experience?*
- *How do you support young people to find the strengths in what they already know and what they can already do?*
- *Young people may not be clear about their own interests in learning. How do you approach this?*
- *How do you learn new strategies to do this better or differently?*

Differentiated and Personalised Curriculum

Differentiated curriculum was a common thread in interviews when staff discussed learning choices support and it was described in a number of ways. First, in terms of what young people themselves wanted in their learning and also in terms of staff having to manage a wide range of levels and needs in any group of young people at any given time. Staff highlighted the value of, *"having a fairly good grasp of where every student is at in their learning" (INT 12)*. Recognising that young people have different learning needs at varying stages of involvement in the program highlighted the need for differentiated and personalised curriculum.

> *Other things that work is building the stages. When they first come in, I think they want a different kind of learning than when they've been there for a while. And as they relax into the system and start to trust you, you can ask for different things. (INT 04)*

Critical reflection for self-awareness and awareness of others:

Differentiated & personalised curriculum

- *What strategies and tools do you use to differentiate and personalise curriculum for young people in your learning group?*
- *Who supports and challenges you in developing skills in this area?*
- *Is this an area of professional learning that would be beneficial for you in your work with young people?*
- *Do you have particular skills or expertise in this aspect of practice that you could share in your staff team?*
- *When did you last brainstorm with colleagues about fresh approaches to personal learning plans?*

Ann Morgan, Ph.D.

Questioning the Purpose of Education

Questioning the purpose of education was identified as the final common thread identified in the stories of educators considering learning choices support. Traditional notions of education are challenged through the privileging of relationships in flexi schools. Narrowing conceptions of education in current national and international reform agendas do not meet the changing needs of young people, especially those who experience multiple complexity and social exclusion (Dwyer & Wyn, 2001; Smyth et al., 2004; Wyn, 2008). In interviews with staff, education was perceived in a holistic way recognising that all aspects of the young people's lives need to be developed and strengthened.

> *I could come in as a teacher, and I probably did come into this organisation with teacher thinking "Oh learning is great and having an education is great" and if I offer them this gift and they say they want it and they get it, which they did, then everything else will fall into place. And I quickly learnt that it doesn't. You've got to build all the other parts of that young person at the same time, or the gift that they're taking from you and that they're gifting themselves too, it'll fall over. It'll fall over because the other things haven't been looked at along the way. (INT 10)*

Educational outcomes such as personal development and growth, setting aspirational goals and the ability to get along with others, were seen as worthwhile and valid outcomes of education.

> *Give them a bit of an awareness of who they are, where everything fits in the whole scheme of things and open their minds up to, to new things and possibilities that they can achieve in their lives, whether a career, whether you know trying to read, trying to get along with other people. (INT 08)*

Critical Reflection for self-awareness and awareness of others:

Questioning the purpose of education

- *How do you understand and define teaching and learning and the broader concept of education?*
- *Have you ever written a personal philosophy of education? Spend some time doing this and discuss your ideas with a colleague.*
- *How have your own experiences of education shaped your personal philosophy? You may wish to consider both positive and negative experiences in your reflection.*

Positive Relationship Support

Positive relationship support was the fourth category identified in interview data analysis. Interviewees highlighted a range of effective ways of working with young people. Common threads in this category can be seen in figure 6.

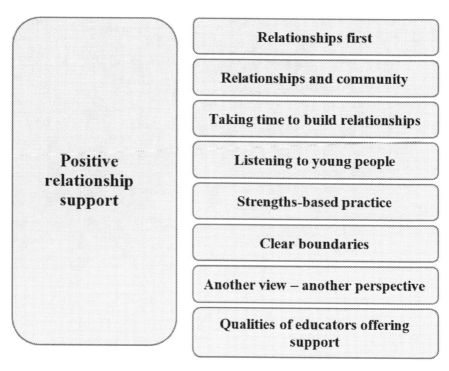

Figure 6. Common threads in positive relationship support.

Relationships First

Common threads in *positive relationship support* again included an emphasis on prioritising *relationships first*. One staff member reiterated the centrality of relationships in her work with young people.

> *One thing that I find really helpful with the [work] is relationships first. You know, you need to build that relationship. If you do not feel that relationship with a young person, it doesn't work and it's a constant thing you are constantly building that relationship with them. (INT 13)*

Educators also talked about the need to develop rapport with young people through really getting to know them. *"That's the rapport. That's the big one with these kids. I mean if you don't have rapport, forget it, you're not going to do it" (INT 2)*. Also important was taking a personal interest in them — *"Humour works. A real interest in them works" (INT 04)*. Being aware of the young people's particular interests and passions was viewed as significant. *"You always focus on what their interests are first, they're the most important people in the world" (INT 14)*.

Staff felt that emphasising relationships first and curriculum second supported young people to feel more comfortable and to be more confident. For educators, patience, acceptance, and understanding were required to enter into an *"authentic relationship with young people" (INT 16)*. Where educators viewed young people as equals, they sensed the young people felt respected.

Critical reflection for self-awareness and awareness of others:

Relationships first

- *What does RAPPORT mean to you?*
- *How do you intentionally develop rapport with your young people?*
- *How do you use humour?*
- *How do you show a real interest in young people?*
- *In what situations do you lose patience, acceptance or understanding?*
- *How do you work through this in an honest, authentic way?*
- *Who supports you in this process and gives you feedback on your practice?*

Relationships and Community

Relationships were perceived by some educators to be connected to community. This was the second common thread for the category of *positive relationship support*. The connection between *relationships and community* helped to create a sense of belonging for young people as they gradually felt part of the school community. Relationships and community were linked by a staff member who talked of the impact of this on a young person who had recently left the school.

> *Even when I think of a young person say from last year, who has gone forward and left the school. She has actually benefited by being part of the school because she felt like a member and felt that relationship with the school community. Now I think that that was probably good. (INT 07)*

Another staff member also emphasised the need to link young people into their wider local community, being able to "*see the bigger picture*" *(INT 08)*.

Critical reflection for self-awareness and awareness of others:

Relationships and community

- *How do you intentionally create a learning environment that fosters a sense of belonging?*
- *Who does this really well at your flexi school? Have you ever spent a day working with this person to observe and learn from them?*
- *What connections to your local community do you support young people to foster? Who decides which connections to make?*
- *Can you recall a situation or learning experience that enabled young people to "see the bigger picture"?*
- *What happened and what influence did this have on young people in your care?*

Taking Time to Build Relationships

Taking time to build relationships was the third common thread in positive relationship support. Educators recognised that it takes time to build relationships with young people, particularly where those young people are returning to formal education and are facing complex issues in their lives. They understood this relationship building process might take considerable time. Educators acknowledged that there was a need to *"hang in with young people over time" (INT 03)*, that building rapport with young people occurs over time and does not happen overnight. Time is needed to not only develop an initial relationship with a young person but to sustain that relationships over their time at the flexi school.

> *I build rapport over time, which is one of the troubles in [mainstream settings], I could hardly build rapport because, before I knew it, there'd be another class [arriving] . . . Whereas here, you really have a chance to build [rapport]. (INT 04)*

Critical reflection for self-awareness and awareness of others:

Taking time to build relationships

- *How do you take time for yourself? What stops you from doing this regularly? What could you do to change this?*
- *How might the idea of self-care translate into the ways you take time with young people?*
- *Who in your flexi school is very skilled at taking time to be present with young people?*
- *Have you ever observed this colleague working with young people over a longer period of time? How could you organise this?*
- *Have you ever asked this person about the intentional strategies they use to do this?*
- *Could you convene a staff discussion on this topic to share ideas and practice in your team?*

Listening to Young People

The fourth common thread in *positive relationship support* is *listening to young people*. Educators saw the consequence of listening to young people in a range of ways. When educators practised listening attentively, young people had a sense of being valued. The importance of having regular and relevant conversations with young people was seen by a number of educators as part of their daily work. *"I can just sit and listen and talk and I'm quite content with that if [young] people want to do that"* (INT 07). Another staff member saw themselves as a sounding board for young people.

> *I like to talk, you know and I think working with these young students and young people, they don't have that opportunity to talk to people – to talk to parents, to talk to their own family, so I'm there as a sounding board for them. I'm there initiating conversations with them. (INT 08)*

For another educator, valuing conversations with young people around life experiences rather than overemphasising academic learning was essential because that was where the opportunity for positive relationship support became apparent.

> *. . . but it's in conversation and it's around ah, life experiences, so, if we can turn a young person round from being an introverted or internalising aggressive person into a relaxed, pleasant young person. (INT 05)*

Critical reflection for self-awareness and awareness of others:

Listening to young people

- *Who are the young people you find most challenging to listen to?*
- *What is it that they trigger within you?*
- *Have you observed another staff member who is especially good at listening to that same young person?*
- *Ask this colleague to list or tell you four things they love or value about this particular young person.*
- *Look for strengths and potential in young people who challenge you.*

Strengths-Based Practice

Strengths-based practice was identified as the fifth common thread in *positive relationship support*. This was expressed by a number of staff in terms of seeing the potential in the young people and being prepared to take risks with them. *"I've explained to them very, very openly that I'm taking a risk because I think they have the potential"* (INT 04). One educator expressed her own preference for working within a strengths perspective with young people.

> *I've really found value in that strengths approach in the work and the narrative approach as well. It's really finding out and talking to young people, firstly finding out their story and then bringing the strength perspective to that (INT 06).*

Staff also saw the importance of seeing the dignity of young people and recognising that young people *"like us, want to learn"* (INT 16).

Critical reflection for self-awareness and awareness of others:

Strengths-based practice

- *What have you learnt about strengths-based approaches to working with young people? (McCashen, 2005)*
- *Do you have a positive expectation that young people, like adults, want to learn?*
- *What has shaped your expectations around young people's learning?*
- *In what ways might your expectations be supportive OR limiting of young people's potential?*

Clear Boundaries

Some staff saw that establishing *clear boundaries* was important in their work with young people and this was identified as a common thread in the fourth category of *positive relationship support*. Establishing clear boundaries involved showing and modelling to young people appropriate ways of treating others and confronting or challenging them at times *"to be the best young person they can be" (INT 05)*.

For another educator, clear boundaries were connected to being consistent. Consistency was linked to having a strong relationship with young people, establishing rapport and having some flexibility.

> *[It's] consistency; consistency is the best method, no matter how hard it is, how mean you look and um, brain strain, or boring, or numbing it is, don't give in. That consistency, it teaches young people that this is not acceptable ... consistency is the game with a bit of flexibility. (INT 02)*

Critical reflection for self-awareness and awareness of others:

Clear boundaries

- *When are you most challenged to be consistent with young people?*
- *Are your boundaries clear and do young people understand them?*
- *How do you respond to young people when boundaries are not respected? Who gives you feedback on this aspect of your practice?*
- *Who sets the boundaries in your learning groups with young people?*
- *When did you last facilitate a working agreement with your learning group?*
- *If you are unsure how to do this, who could you ask at your flexi school to support you?*
- *Perhaps you could observe another educator facilitating a working agreement with a group of young people.*

Another View — Another Perspective

Another common thread identified in the data analysis of interviews with educators was the idea of helping to give young people *another view — another perspective*. This may have been in relation to themselves and their identity and sense of self-esteem. It was also discussed in relation to young people recognising their ability through challenging them about what is their best ability, or supporting young people in their own capacity to try a different way in their relationships or in their learning. *"You can give them a nudge and say, 'hey, pull your head in' and try a different way" (INT 02)*.

Seeing a purpose in what they were doing and in what they were learning was one way this common thread was discussed. For example, an educator understood that *"the future is important and that young people can do something for themselves" (INT 07)*. Seeing the bigger picture was also about supporting young people to see a purpose for what they were doing.

> And once they feel safe, then that [academic achievement] happens. And often it's quite slowly and then it's sort of "d, d, d, d, d, d" [sound effect for falling into place]. And if they see a purpose, they want something as well, OK you want to do this, you want to try and achieve this, you must do this, this, this. OK, they see a purpose for it. (INT 09)

Critical reflection for self-awareness and awareness of others:

Another view – another perspective

- *What learning activities have you designed that support young people to take risks in a safe and supportive environment? In what ways do you feel this experience broadened their horizons and view of the world?*
- *How did you evaluate and document this outcome in learning (e.g., young people's stories, group debriefs, pre and post activity survey)?*
- *How do you seek out and listen to other views about your own practice? Who supports you to do this in your role?*
- *How do you actively support adventure-based learning (outdoor education) and experiential learning in your flexi school?*
- *Have young people observed you operating outside of your comfort zone?*

Qualities of Educators Offering Support

The final common thread in the category of *positive relationship support* highlighted the *qualities of educators offering support.* In discussing positive relationship support, a range qualities identified by educators were mentioned in interviews. These qualities included, but were not limited to: wisdom; patience; humour; acceptance; being young at heart; sensitive; caring; understanding; and tolerant, as well as being compassionate and empathetic. These qualities enhance relationships with young people and, over time, support more positive engagement and the provision of relevant and meaningful learning opportunities. Qualities were defined within the context of having positive relationships with young people:

> *I do enjoy having good relationships with young people and I do find it reasonably easy and I think it's because I do see them as an equal, not as someone who needs me or that needs anything really from me except probably patience and acceptance and understanding and things like that. (INT 15)*

Patience was a quality mentioned by another educator in relation to young people.

> *[It's]the patience we have for our students and what we're trying to achieve with them. We're not pushing them to obtain great results. We're not pushing them to be something that they don't want to be. We're giving them the opportunity to grow as a person, to grow as an individual and whatever that individual might be. (INT 08)*

Critical reflection for self-awareness and awareness of others:

Educator qualities

- *What personal qualities are strengths in your practice as an educator?*
- *What personal qualities would you like to foster to support you in the challenging aspects of your practice with young people and colleagues?*

- *What supports you in developing a greater sense of self-awareness?*
- *Who do you seek feedback from in relation to the personal qualities you demonstrate in your work practice?*
- *You may wish to further explore this topic by looking at the section of this book on Personal Dispositions (see Ch.7, p.109)*

PART II

Ways of Working with Colleagues

4

The *Relational Shift* in Working with Colleagues

The primacy of relationships is vitally important within a flexi school learning community. The need to feel comfortable and safe in relationships with colleagues is essential. Staff recognise they need the support of their colleagues to do their work effectively. They also recognise that they need to *offer* support to their colleagues. Developing productive staff relationships is just as critical as developing authentic relationships with young people. Developing supportive staff teams in the work context requires the same shift from task orientation to greater people orientation.

Developing supportive and positive relationships within staff teams occurs over time, through practice and through critical reflection on practice. Three movements in the *relational shift* for educators working collaboratively with colleagues can be seen in figure 7.

1. A Shift Towards Valuing Staff Relationships and Support

Productive relationships among colleagues offers much needed support. The sense of support being enacted in relationships between colleagues was clearly evident in interview and questionnaire data. Support was mentioned in different ways but included practical support, emotional support and professional support. Accessing the expertise of practitioners from other professional disciplines including youth work and community services was crucial for achieving positive outcomes with young people. Staff capacity to contribute to the creation of a culture of offering support and asking for support is a key element of working relationally with colleagues.

In the staff questionnaire, the most important sources of professional support identified by educators was from colleagues at local sites. The relational shift involves staff moving from being an isolated, individual practitioner to being part of a dynamic team. Such a shift requires each educator to accept responsibility for being able to receive support and being willing to offer support to others. This aspect of practice is an important influence on educator identity and development in practice in the context of flexi schools.

2. A Shift Towards Working with the Four Principles with Colleagues

One of the significant features of using the four principles incorporating respect, participation, safe and legal, and honesty is that this model applies equally to young people and adults. It not only guides relationships with young people but also guides relationships between adults who are working together. Negotiating through the four principles assists educators to find common ground with young people as well as with their colleagues. These practices can support educators to work more collaboratively. Collaboration requires enacting respect and the ability to *"be open honest if things aren't working" (INT 01)*. Educators perceived that it was important for young people to be able to see the role modelling of adults using the four principles in relationships with other adults. This modelling offers practical examples of the principles in action. It supports young people to develop their own capacity to negotiate relationships and conflict with their peers and staff in a constructive manner.

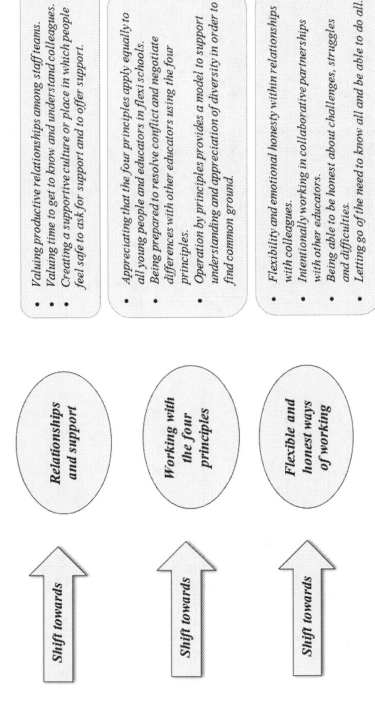

- *Valuing productive relationships among staff teams.*
- *Valuing time to get to know and understand colleagues.*
- *Creating a supportive culture or place in which people feel safe to ask for support and to offer support.*

- *Appreciating that the four principles apply equally to all young people and educators in flexi schools.*
- *Being prepared to resolve conflict and negotiate differences with other educators using the four principles.*
- *Operation by principles provides a model to support understanding and appreciation of diversity in order to find common ground.*

- *Flexibility and emotional honesty within relationships with colleagues.*
- *Intentionally working in collaborative partnerships with other educators.*
- *Being able to be honest about challenges, struggles and difficulties.*
- *Letting go of the need to know all and be able to do all.*

Relationships and support

Working with the four principles

Flexible and honest ways of working

Shift towards

Shift towards

Shift towards

Figure 7. The Relational Shift in working with colleagues – moving from task orientation to greater people orientation.

3. A Shift Towards Flexible and Honest Ways of Working

The flexibility staff experience within their work is viewed as positive. Staff are encouraged to be flexible and try out new ideas in their work with young people. Being able to learn from making mistakes and experiencing failure is a freedom that educators experience and seek to cultivate in their teams. This growth mindset (Dweck, 2006), is captured in comments such as, *"OK let's give this a go"* rather than *"Oh I don't think this is gonna work" (INT 08).*

Honesty with colleagues is evident when staff feel safe to admit they are experiencing difficulties in their work or are struggling to connect with certain young people. In the flexi schools, adults and young people are expected to work within the operation by principles model. This way of working is challenging at times for adults and requires a shift in mindset to incorporate greater flexibility and honesty. Flexibility and honesty are part of the relational culture in flexi schools that has developed between young people and staff. It also influences relationships between educators in terms of their own sense of professional identity as they learn to offer this flexibility and honesty to themselves and their colleagues. A teacher recognised that, unless adults are prepared to be open and honest and have the difficult conversations, it is not realistic to expect young people to do the same. *"We can't ask young people to have a conversation about a difficult thing [and] agree to have a conversation on something that's not working, if we don't." (INT 01)*

Staff expressed a genuine sense that they are working in partnership with other adults, and that they are endeavouring to negotiate and come to some shared understanding and appreciation of difference. When issues of conflict arise between staff there is an expectation within the flexi school culture that staff will make a commitment to work within the four principles with an intention to find common ground. The challenge of differences between adults means that tensions and disagreements are at times, inevitable. However, using the operation by principles model, offers educators a practice framework that can be applied daily. Navigating difference and conflict in more constructive ways requires skills that educators can learn and regularly practise.

5

Stories from Practitioners —
Ways of Working with Colleagues

This section of the book explores ways of working with colleagues through the data analysis of interviews with educators. Educators' perceptions of effective ways of working with colleagues will be presented through extracts organised in three categories (see figure 8).

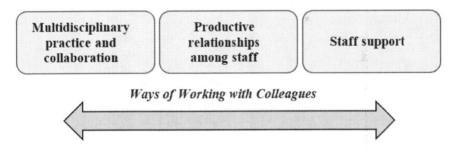

Figure 8. Ways of working with colleagues.

Within each of these three categories, a number of common threads are presented. Questions that prompt critical reflection are linked to each common thread. You are invited to use these questions to assist individual reflection or to support discussions with supervisors, mentors and staff teams.

As previously mentioned, a central feature of critical reflection compared with other models of reflection is that underlying assumptions, values and beliefs are brought to reflective processes in order to be unsettled (Fook & Gardner, 2007) and where appropriate, challenged for improved practice. These assumptions, values and beliefs are influenced and shaped by our worldview and our social/economic/cultural positioning. The purpose of critical reflection is to bring to our awareness those points of struggle — those challenging places in which we find ourselves stuck. It supports the development of "critical awareness and emotional insight alongside self-knowledge and deepening understanding of the other" (West, 2010, p. 66). The possibilities for transformation and liberation in our thinking and actions in practice will hopefully assist us to be more effective in our work with colleagues. This transformation has implications for how challenging issues in practice can be addressed constructively.

Multidisciplinary Practice and Collaboration

In interviews with educators, *multidisciplinary practice and collaboration* was talked about in a range of ways. Figure 9 shows the common threads within this first category.

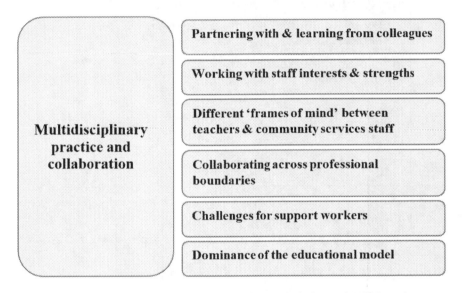

Figure 9. Common threads in multidisciplinary practice and collaboration.

The perceptions of educators about multidisciplinary practice showed a link between "doing their work" and "social participation". Multidisciplinary practice was enacted and experienced in staff relationships that were generally characterised as being supportive, helpful, a resource for practice, comfortable and open. Some staff had experienced multidisciplinary practice in other work contexts and it was not new to them. For others, it was quite a contrast to previous work contexts and required a shift in understanding.

Ann Morgan, Ph.D.

Partnering with and Learning from Colleagues

Partnering with and learning from colleagues was understood in a range of ways. Some educators recognised the benefit of working across professional boundaries and experienced support through drawing on the expertise and complementary skills of educators from other professional backgrounds. Sharing knowledge across professional disciplines occurred regularly for some staff.

> *I think the biggest thing has been collaboration. Collaboration with other workers - really sharing on a very regular basis. You know, how's it going? What's going on? Yeah. Collaboration with the other workers here and really sharing of our knowledges, you know, across disciplines, across learning areas. (INT 01)*

Critical reflection for self-awareness and awareness of others:

Partnering with & learning from colleagues

- *Have you had experience of working in contexts with multidisciplinary teams?*
- *What have you learnt from colleagues from other professional disciplines?*
- *Has regular sharing with educators from different professional backgrounds supported your own professional learning? In what ways has this occurred?*
- *What do you think are the challenges of working in multidisciplinary teams?*

Working with Staff Interests and Strengths

The second common thread in *multidisciplinary practice and collaboration* was *working with staff interests and strengths*. This was particularly relevant in mobile outreach situations where the staffing generally consisted of a youth worker and a teacher with up to 15 young people. Boundaries between roles were not as marked in these settings with flexibility for educators to draw on the strengths of each staff person rather than strictly working according to roles such as teacher and youth worker. There was a sense of *"blending of each other's strengths. A sort of balancing" (INT 08)* and working where the strengths are. Educators recognised the benefits of working with their own interests, strengths and passion. They believed that young people were more likely to be influenced positively when staff could work within their strengths and interests. The focus in these situations was still clearly on the needs of the young people and how these needs could be most effectively met. In larger sites educators made reference to drawing on the strengths and interests of colleagues, even those from other sites, especially in relation to planning units of work for young people.

> Those that are keen to do it will do it [sharing ideas]. And by now, like I've got in my head say the name of five people who I would contact about "xyz". And that I know are keen to talk about that. And they typically the ones who also put things on the forum [online sharing space]. (INT 04)

Critical reflection for self-awareness and awareness of others:

Identifying staff interests & strengths

- *What are your own strengths that you bring to your practice with young people and colleagues?*
- *Have you experienced working to your own strengths and encouraging other colleagues to work with their strengths?*
- *How do you contribute to the culture of sharing ideas and experiences of practice within your own team?*
- *What are the blocks that you have experienced in working across professional boundaries? Have you found strategies to get through these blocks?*

Different Frames of Mind between Teachers and Community Services Staff

A third common thread in *multidisciplinary practice and collaboration* was the notion of *different frames of mind between teachers and community services staff.* Some educators talked about this as a learning opportunity. They had been unfamiliar with the idea of a practice framework that was commonly used by staff from a community services background. This awareness caused one particular teacher to reflect on developing their own practice framework and to consider how it might influence their work with young people.

> *I've always been interested in ecology . . . I guess that's part of the philosophical framework. It's kind of a framework for my work . . . in coming here – you know – "what's your framework?" Wow, social workers talk about their framework – I went ooh! What's my framework? I wonder what it is . . . (INT 01)*

The different frames of mind were at times also expressed in language. For example, among youth workers, social workers and community workers, the term "young people" or "young person", was most commonly used in practice. Teachers in mainstream contexts generally use the term "students". In the research context, while young people was the term most commonly adopted, some teachers used "students" or "kids" to refer to the young people. One teacher found himself reflecting on this language and recognised that youth work discourse had influenced the wider educator discourse in the network context in a positive way.

> *So their [youth workers] language was a different discourse. It really is significantly different to the language used in education. And it will be interesting to see in the [flexi school sites] what will be the language incorporated. There's already, not a conflict, but there's already a tension around the word "young people" and "students". Um, and I think, I probably have been sold on the word young people. (INT 05)*

The teacher showed understanding of the philosophical underpinnings of using the term young people as a more dignified expression of equality and valuing of the person, rather than a term that can denote a different level in traditional power dynamics.

The different frames of mind between teachers and community services workers, was also highlighted by a youth worker who had observed that certain ways of speaking, such as using directive language and the use of imperatives, and certain body language used by some teachers, tended to reinforce more authoritarian or traditional roles. While this was not generally widespread amongst all teachers in the context, it had come to the attention of the youth worker. For example, during a small group meeting, a teacher stood in front of a group in the classroom at the whiteboard while young people sat on the floor. The youth worker preferred to be part of a circle when she was facilitating a discussion with young people. This meant she would deliberately place herself at the same physical level alongside young people. This highlights a different awareness between a particular teacher and a youth worker regarding non-verbal communication with young people and power dynamics that can become apparent through the physical environment. The youth worker recognised that difference was not necessarily problematic if awareness accompanies the choices made for specific purposes in certain situations.

> *But I do notice that there's different ways that the people who have a background in education would occasionally approach things than people with a background in social work or community services. And I'm not necessarily saying one way is wrong or right but there's definitely differences and when I first came to watch those different interactions, yea it was interesting to find where I fit . . . it's just the whole manner, the body language and everything, um, is very different. And there were times when I was wondering you know, now where is it in a teaching degree do they even teach about body language? And you might be saying it in a nice way but what is your body language expressing? (INT 06)*

Several teachers acknowledged that youth workers provided a very good sounding board for them as they sought advice, support and ideas from both trained and untrained youth workers. Teachers perceived that youth workers' different experiences of life and work offered another perspective which enhanced the relationships of teachers with young people.

> *Youth workers are gold, 'cause their skills . . . their skills in just working through what to say to a young person [that] is appropriate. And as a teacher, I've learnt a lot and my experience has given me a lot ... we've got some teachers who were youth workers and [I often] go "Is this appropriate?" or "what should I do?" Cause if I think I'm not right or if I'm a bit worried about something I would definitely go and ask if not the boss, then someone I know who has that experience. (INT 14)*

Critical reflection for self-awareness and awareness of others:

Learning from others with different 'frames of mind'

- *At any time in your practice have you been aware of differences in mindset between teachers and other educators from community services backgrounds?*
- *When this has been challenging in your staff team, who do you seek support from on your team?*
- *Are you able to ask for support and offer support to staff from a range of different professional backgrounds?*
- *How do you have open and honest conversations about these issues within your staff teams?*

Collaborating Across Professional Boundaries

The fourth common thread in *multidisciplinary practice and collaboration* was *collaborating across professional boundaries*. In some instances where this had occurred, educators had developed a common vocabulary in their practice that proved useful. The valuing of training and study, whether done individually or in teams, provided opportunities for educators to be supported and challenged in their current concepts around working with young people.

> *Another thing I guess is that we've specifically done training together. So that we can relate our own discipline areas to the training that we're doing and it forms a communication arc across to other colleagues who have different backgrounds. So really specifically, the teacher educators communicate with the social worker educators. We did training that gave us ... a common vocabulary so that did really help. (INT 01)*

Some teachers stated that their understanding of youth work practice was not clear and that greater clarity in this area would be advantageous. *"I think it would be good if both teachers and youth workers, if everybody sort of knew what the others were doing it would be pretty handy"* (INT 12).

Networking across agencies was also identified by a few participants as an enhancement to practice. This tended to be a common aspect of practice for those educators from community services background but not so evident for teachers (Edwards, 2004; Friesen, Finney, & Krentz, 1999). The general sense from teachers interviewed was that teachers who are mostly not experienced in youth work and social work practice, need to draw on aspects of both domains for their work in this context as they are complementary and support enhanced outcomes for young people (Edwards, 2005).

> *Maybe they [teachers] should be given lots of in-service about that [youth work practice]. Cause I know their skills are more of a social work realm and teachers are educators, but you've got to kind of cover both, but I'm not experienced it that. (INT 14)*

Critical reflection for self-awareness and awareness of others:

Collaborating across professional boundaries

- *What experiences of collaboration across professional disciplines have you had?*
- *What were the benefits of this kind of collaboration?*
- *Are you aware of not always understanding the perspective of educators from other professional disciplines? What have you done to remedy this? Perhaps you could raise this as a topic at a team meeting?*
- *Can you identify one aspect of your practice that has improved because of your collaboration with educators from other professional disciplines? Describe how this occurred.*

Challenges for Support Workers

When discussing *multidisciplinary practice and collaboration*, a fifth common thread identified was *challenges for support workers*, particularly in relation to equity issues. While the general feeling towards multidisciplinary practice and collaboration from the interview participants was positive, some participants highlighted that the common boundaries between support workers such as teacher aides and education support workers in mainstream contexts were not always as clearly apparent in the flexi school context.

> *There are times where maybe a lot has been expected of them. Or we take them for granted, perhaps … with a teacher you've got to do your planning, you've got to do all the background stuff and sometimes it might seem that they are expected to do that. But I think they [support workers] take on an awful lot, outside their role here. And I don't know if I would actually like to be in their shoes, being a teacher aide. (INT 14)*

With the emphasis on developing safe and supportive relationships with young people, support staff (i.e., youth workers, teacher aides, and other support workers) engage in a dynamic way alongside teachers in the work with young people. Some support workers have the advantage of being young people themselves, while others are very familiar with the local community and cultural groups — both socio-economically and in terms of the ethnic or Indigenous dimensions of culture. The social and cultural capital of these educators is recognised on the ground in a day to day capacity in interactions with young people and colleagues. However, the limitations of an industrial award that delineates between educators in terms of formal qualifications and their associated rates of pay and number of hours/weeks worked, but which does not formally recognise social and cultural capital through economic remuneration, can be problematic at times. The social and cultural capital of support workers were recognised as essential elements of practice in the flexi schools' context. Some staff felt that this work should also be valued in an economic sense, given its very significant contribution to the effectiveness of the work in the context.

The teachers, you know they do the relationship stuff and the bit of youth work and stuff but their focus is pretty clear, here you're a teacher this is what you're gonna do. Whereas the others, the youth workers, the social workers and those people, it's not that clear. It's pretty muddy, because they do, do teaching, because they use teaching, they'll take classes. They'll take kids out and do stuff, so they'll link it to the curriculum or they'll use that as a vehicle to move it along to the next thing to work out some issues with some young people. So it gets really blurry. And then I s'pose there's pay issues, there's holiday issues. There's all those sorts of things that come into play that makes it very muddy. (INT 12)

This lack of recognition can affect the promotion and valuing of multidisciplinary practice and collaboration through power differences (Rueda & Monzo, 2002).

Critical reflection for self-awareness and awareness of others:

Challenges for support workers

- *Are you conscious of some of the challenges faced by support workers in the flexi schools' context?*
- *How can awareness of power dynamics within teams help to create a more supportive environment? What can you do to contribute to a collaborative and respectful team culture?*
- *Are you conscious of your personal power and/or the power inherent within your own role?*
- *How can you bring your awareness to differences in power dynamics in order to maintain the dignity of every person on your team?*

Dominance of the Education Model

The issue of power differences leads into the final common thread in *multidisciplinary practice and collaboration*, the *dominance of the education model* in flexi schools. Some participants commented that multidisciplinary practice had decreased over the years and was not as strong now since the schools have become larger, with a greater number of teachers employed.

> *There's not a lot of people from different backgrounds. This is very much a teaching place now. It's very a teacher dominated thing and teacher aides are doing the work of teachers. They're what you would call a youth worker but that's a youth support coordinator whose role is quite different. Like they work, they work with a particular case load for example, like eight or ten, and they don't take on any new clients once they've reached that – like they're very careful about their load and the other part of their role is to be sort of pro-active and access other programs which will run here, right? So we don't really have a youth worker in the sense of somebody who'd be hanging out or something. A teacher can't turn around and say to a youth worker "Do you mind just going and sitting with them for a couple of hours" and you haven't got that sort of, it's a different, it's on a different level. (INT 10)*

In the past it was felt that the youth worker role was often a voice of challenge for teaching staff. In many instances the advocacy role of youth workers was dynamic. In the network context where the primary focus has been on reengaging and enfranchising young people in and through education, multidisciplinary practice offers teachers new ways of working with young people. Many community services workers are trained to recognise that young people need support in a variety of complex areas of their lives, not only in formal learning choices. Without the holistic approach offered by community services workers providing other practice frameworks, something has been lost for young people who experience multiple complexities in their lives.

There have been in the past youth workers who have been employed as youth workers to like just you know be here, part of the place. [Previous youth workers] ... would have a big overview of all of the students. And they would challenge, they would challenge teaching staff. They would keep that balance right. They would say "look, this, you know, the way you're approaching that student, because they're not participating in a classroom they have to go home, there's more to that young person". (INT 10)

A staff member recognised that the accountability measures for teachers had increased dramatically over time with regard to curriculum, assessment, administration and other dimensions of professionalism now imposed on teachers. *"Teachers too now, [pause] are very busy - they're busy with the teaching, they're busy with the education. Now, the accountability measures are much more" (INT 10).* This increased accountability, combined with the diminishing number of community services workers employed in some sites, is a potential threat to the continuation of vibrant multidisciplinary practice in the flexi schools context.

Critical reflection for self-awareness and awareness of others:

Dominance of the education model

Are you familiar with the idea of "deschooling" (Ivan Illich)?

- *What does this mean for you in your role and daily practice with young people?*
- *There is a tension at times in terms of working relationally with disenfranchised young people and the reality that our sites are schools with accountabilities to funding bodies. How do you deal with this tension?*
- *Have you considered your own values, ideals, assumptions and what you understand to be the nature and purpose of education?*

What model of education prevails?

- *Are you aware of different perspectives on models of education within your staff team? In what forum can you have these discussions?*
- *Look at Sir Kenneth Robinson's talks on education paradigms and creativity:*
  https://www.youtube.com/watch?v=zDZFcDGpL4U
  http://www.ted.com/talks/ken_robinson_says_schools_kill_creativity?language=en
- *Perhaps these could be the focus of your personal reflection or a team discussion. What questions might these raise for you and your team?*

Productive Relationships Among Colleagues

Productive relationships among colleagues was the second category identified in ways of working with staff. Educators talked about the importance of developing productive relationships in a variety of ways. Figure 10 shows the common threads in this category.

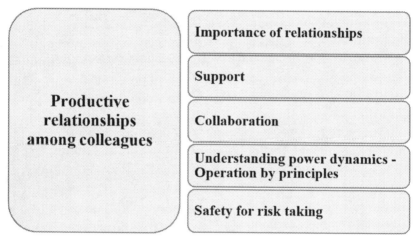

Figure 10. Common threads in productive relationships among colleagues.

The five common threads above are explored within this category of *productive relationships among colleagues*. Questions that prompt critical self-reflection are linked to each common thread. These questions can be used to guide self-reflection or to support reflective practice with supervisors, mentors and in staff teams. Remember, critical reflection that challenges underlying values, beliefs and assumptions can occur in a variety of ways and in a range of settings.

Importance of Relationships

When considering the *importance of relationships*, certain personal qualities were highlighted by staff as being significant. These qualities included openness, honesty, patience, and friendliness. Educators indicated that when these qualities were cultivated, productive and safe relationships within staff teams were developed.

A number of staff felt that relationships with staff and with young people were bound together in the notion of community. A certain degree of accountability to the school community occurs as a result of working in a relational manner. One participant talked about relationships in the context of community in the following way:

> *I think that relationship is bound up with the idea of community. If we hold relationships as important, I think that the natural outcome is the whole community idea. But within the community a number of relationships are actually made, so support, I suppose for when a staff member comes in - that the relationships are started within the actual school community. They [staff] have a responsibility as well as the young people have an opportunity to make some sort of relationship that can be a helpful relationship. (INT 07)*

Several participants felt that relationships were the most important aspect of the work. Through developing positive relationships, trust increases. With trust comes safety. A number of staff felt comfortable and safe in their relationships with their colleagues and were able to ask a lot of questions when necessary and they felt closely supported.

> *I guess within the workers, I know I was very open and up front that I was a new practitioner, I'm gonna have a lot of questions and just working in this environment I feel completely comfortable to just stick up my hand and say, "I don't know what you're talking about, can you help out?" And so to have a team of people, that you're that comfortable with - and I also think that it's great that within that team we've got a range of people. There are people who have been here for years and years and who are a bit older and more experienced and then there's*

> *a group of, I guess younger workers as well. And we all bring different things to the table as well so we can all support each other in different areas. (INT 06)*

It was also noted that, if staff are living and modelling the importance of relationships with each other, this modelling filters down to what happens with the young people:

> *So it's the relationship building [among staff], which is quite ironic, because when I started here I would never have thought that would be the case. I didn't really know what to expect to be quite honest. And so those relationships, which I suppose filters down to what happens with the kids . . . 'cause that's where the trust comes. (INT 12)*

Critical reflection for self-awareness and awareness of others:

Importance of relationships

- *What has been your experience of relationships within your staff team?*
- *When some relationships within your team are strained, how do you reconnect and build bridges to restore relationships?*
- *What activities does your staff team do that specifically have the purpose of building productive relationships?*
- *Who supports you when you are struggling in relationship with other members of your team?*
- *How do you rebuild trust when relationships have been strained?*

Support

Support was another common thread in *productive relationships among colleagues*. It was mentioned in a number of different ways — from the practical support offered on the ground on a day to day basis, to the emotional support that staff experienced in their relationships with colleagues. One participant perceived that, *"there was a mentality within the [flexi schools] about nurturing and making sure people [staff] are feeling comfortable and that they're OK" (INT 09)*. Another participant felt that experiences of negativity and "backstabbing" were notable in their absence and that there was a genuine sense of respect and support.

> *I think it's the staff. Because you can always bounce ideas off them and everything like that … and just the friendliness. There's no backstabbing or stuff or anything like that, it's all, you know if you've got issues, put the issues on the table. (INT 11)*

Support was also discussed in terms of the professional support staff felt when they were able to draw on the expertise of educators from other disciplines and from those who had significant experience from working in the context over a longer period of time. The experience of mentoring was positively mentioned by a number of participants as well as the opportunity to *"be around excellent people, excellent adults" (INT 10)* and in the process of employment in the early days, *"of hanging around for a while" (INT 10)*.

Critical reflection for self-awareness and awareness of others:

Asking for support and offering support

- *Are you able to ask for support and offer support within your staff team?*
- *If this is problematic for you, what processes are available to you within the wider organisation?*
- *How honest are you able to be within your team about issues that you are struggling with in your practice?*
- *Do you seek advice from a supervisor within the organisation or from an external supervisor?*
- *What other strategies for self-care and support do you use?*

Ann Morgan, Ph.D.

Collaboration

The third common thread in the category of *productive relationships among colleagues* was collaboration. *Collaboration* was spoken about in terms of having *"a strong working team, a sense of cohesion and shared vision" (INT 03)*. Staff felt that there needed to be a sense of unity and a *"solid team for a place to flourish" (INT 13)*. The development of a sense of team partly occurred as a result of *"sharing on a regular basis" (INT 01)*. For example, this sharing occurred formally in morning meetings, afternoon debriefs and at staff meetings, and also informally through giving time to incidental, work-related conversation and sharing.

In the questionnaire data there was a strong sense that collaboration was important for planning and problem solving. Staff generally felt that more collaboration would be preferable. Overall, staff held positive expectations that their peers would be supportive and respectful in answering their questions. Staff felt a much stronger sense of collaboration at a local level, whereas there were quite mixed responses towards collaboration at a wider level across the network of flexi schools. Generally, staff did not have an awareness of the expertise of other staff across the network of flexi schools. At a local level, they were more aware of their peers' expertise that could support collaboration in their workplace. Of interest, in staff responses in the data, were two distinct yet differing ideas about collaboration. Figure 11 highlights two distinct ideas about collaboration.

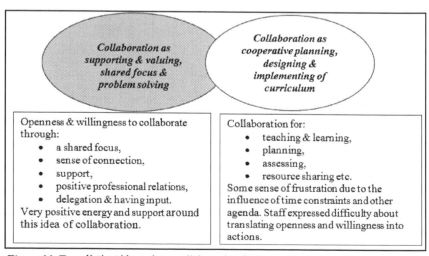

Figure 11. Two distinct ideas about collaboration from questionnaire data.

In keeping with the first notion of collaboration, one respondents' comment was that:

> The staff at my [school] are very professional and supportive in every aspect of the [school] focus. Most matters/concerns are openly discussed & everyone's input is constructive and valued. Achievements are acknowledged and celebrated. I feel valued and my contributions across all aspects are of a high standard due to the staff and the common focus our staff share. (Questionnaire Response 2 – QR2)

This sense of collaboration as support and shared focus in problem solving was reiterated by another respondent who said that *"Everyone is willing to collaborate and share information or assist at any point. It is great" (QR10)*. Finally, a third respondent with a similar perception of collaboration stated:

> Overall I'm greatly impressed by the openness to collaborate, to share many facets of [school] activities. The staff at my [school] are highly skilled, intelligent, committed professionals. There are little difficulties with ego or power issues. This is one of the best staff experiences I have known. (QR19)

In contrast, the following written responses from the questionnaire captured the other understanding of collaboration as cooperative planning and implementation of curriculum. These comments included some level of awareness of the limitations of time: *"Collaboration is a big part of the way we work. Our challenge is finding the time to do collaborative work from planning to delivery"* (QR6). One educator commented that:

> As an unsubstantiated generalisation, staff are happy to collaborate verbally but have difficulty transforming the verbs into actions. I suppose I see it as giving 'lip-service' where nothing actually eventuates. This is probably because of a lack of release/free time. (QR4)

Another educator expressed a sense of frustration in the written comments stating that:

> When it [collaboration] happens it is very good (we are highly qualified!). There is not enough time and room for the actual interesting stuff, for example, us (rather than faraway scientists) exploring social-emotional, science, math, how-to-issues. Much of our meetings are 'wasted' on some other organisation's paper needs, not ours. Support team admin needs, appear to take priority over ours and they don't listen to our need. (QR5)

The distinction between two different ideas about collaboration was evident in another respondent's comment stating that:

> Staff seem willing to share resources but I'm not sure of the level of collaborative planning in terms of classroom stuff. All staff make meaningful contributions into how school runs in other aspects. (QR14)

Some comments on collaboration also included a sense of the importance of relationships in doing the work: *"A collaborative staff is critical to our work at this [school site]. In an environment such as this one, isolation of staff members is extremely counter-productive"* (QR17). Similarly, the notion of collaboration as supportive relationships was expressed in the following comments:

> Collaboration is best achieved when work staff have a history of working together. This friendship is building so the collaboration is improving. The staff are very good and a pleasure to work with. (QR15)
>
> The work is very challenging at a personal level. I believe that we survive individually because we share our experiences and problem solve collaboratively. Young people can contribute through their generosity of spirit. The sense of belonging here can be healing for staff and young people alike. (QR18)

Critical reflection for self-awareness and awareness of others:

Collaboration

- *In what ways do you collaborate within your team?*
- *Have you experienced or identified the two different notions of collaboration described above?*
- *What is your understanding of collaboration?*
- *Do you feel that you give enough time and energy to this aspect of your practice?*
- *What are the blocks to collaboration for you personally?*
- *What possible strategies for developing a more collaborative team culture can you envisage and enact?*

Understanding Power Dynamics
— Operation by Principles

The fourth common thread identified in the second category of *productive relationships among staff* was *understanding power dynamics — operation by principles*. The four principles are respect, participation, safe and legal, and honesty. Using the principles requires negotiation to find *common ground*. This requires a shift in power dynamics between adults and young people, and between educators. As previously mentioned, there was a strong sense that the four principles were for everybody and did not only apply to young people. Younger educators expressed a feeling of being valued and respected by older, more experienced educators. One experienced educator commented that working with the four principles can sometimes *"impact badly"*. Between staff who may have *"a different view of how others are working"*, which can create tensions and disagreements. These differences were not seen by the experienced educator as overly problematic. She had realistic expectations that differences occur and adopted a practical approach requiring daily problem solving of challenging issues. *"You try every point of the compass until you find one that works"* (INT 10).

Critical reflection for self-awareness and awareness of others:

Understanding power dynamics — operation by principles

- *What has informed your understanding of power dynamics?*
- *Have you ever felt disempowered?*
- *What was the situation and how did it influence you personally?*
- *Are you aware of the ways you exercise power with young people and colleagues? How do you understand and enact operation by principles?*
- *Do you regularly seek feedback on your use of power and your understanding of operation by principles from young people and colleagues who have observed your practice?*

Safety for Risk Taking

Finally, *productive relationships among staff* was identified in terms of *safety for risk taking*. Several educators who were interviewed felt able to take risks, try something creative, and *"run with new ideas" (INT 11)*. The sense of being able to *"have a go; who cares if it stuffs up; relationships are the most important thing" (INT 12)* appears to enable staff to learn from mistakes and not be afraid of the risks associated with innovation. Educators felt enabled to admit mistakes and one person commented that, *"the respect and the chance to do better and learn from your mistakes has been genuinely practised" (INT 04)*. Genuinely using the four principles was important in developing productive relationships among staff and a climate that supported safety for risk taking.

Critical reflection for self-awareness and awareness of others:

Safety for risk taking

- *What kind of risks have you taken in your work with young people?*
- *What contributed to your own sense of safety to risk trying something new?*
- *Do you work collaboratively with others when you are trying something new with young people?*
- *Have you experienced disappointment or frustration when you have tried something innovative and it was not successful with the young people?*
- *Who supported you in this process? What did you have to let go of in order to work through this challenge?*

Staff Support

The third category evident in *staff relationships and support* was *staff support*. Common threads within this category can be seen below (see figure 12).

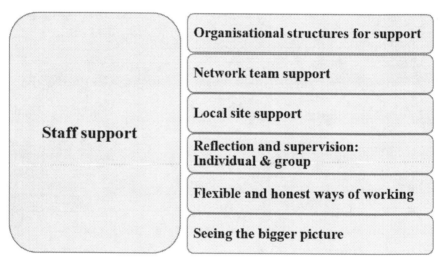

Figure 12. Common threads in learning choices support.

Organisational Structures for Support

Interview participants identified a range of *organisational structures for support* of staff in their work. These included regular meetings such as: morning meetings; staff meetings; community and learning choices meetings; staff days for strategic review and planning; debriefs; induction days; whole staff days; and supervision meetings. These organisational structures were used by staff at different times and for different purposes. Preferences for some options over others were expressed depending on individuals' circumstances and needs. There was generally a high level of satisfaction expressed by staff in relation to the range of options for staff support that were available across the flexi schools.

Critical reflection for self-awareness and awareness of others:

Organisational structures for support

- *What structures for support do you make use of on a regular basis?*
- *Do you have a formal or informal support role with other staff at your site?*
- *How do you ensure you have a voice in the support structures set up within your flexi school?*
- *Do you set your own support goals prior to participating in supervision meetings? How could you be more proactive in terms of your own support needs?*

Network Team Support

The second common thread identified in the interview data related to staff support was the role offered by the *network support team*. At the time this study was conducted, the support team comprised a range of multidisciplinary professionals with specific realms of responsibility, offering support in the following areas: learning choices; child protection; human resource management; identity and formation; induction and professional development; special needs; administration; and a range of other support needs identified by educators through leaders in sites. This team worked across the five school sites participating in this study. Features of the support offered by this team that were identified by staff included a strong emphasis on relationships. Relational practice was often expressed through the sense of availability of the team and the principal to staff. Regarding face-to-face contact, the following was expressed: *"I mean [the principal] has no hesitation if you have a problem that you need to meet face to face he'll book a ticket and come" (INT 08)*. Regular contact by telephone was mentioned by an educator in a regional location. *"I know I can ring [the principal] at the drop of a hat. I know I've got some really good rapport with [the principal]" (INT 02)*. Educators generally expressed confidence in the willingness and capacity of the network support team to assist them in their work, despite the challenges of distance and multiple campuses. Only one interviewee expressed hesitancy to approach support team staff due to the high demand on the team's time across sites.

Critical reflection for self-awareness and awareness of others:

Network team support

- *Are you aware of the support available to you through your network support team?*
- *What are the benefits for staff at your site to have support offered through the network team?*
- *How do you ensure that network team hear and understand the needs of staff at a local site level? In what forums does this occur?*
- *Do you feel you can access the support from your network team easily? If not, what might you do to address this situation?*

Local Site Support

The third common thread in *staff support* identified in interviews with educators was *local site support*. It encompassed a range of aspects such as support offered by colleagues on a one to one basis and through the support of the larger staff team.

> *Well I think having a really good strong working team is really supportive and that's been really useful over the time ... but when we've got good regular supervision, and we're working as a team and we've got sort of, that sense of cohesion, and shared vision, then it's fine. (INT 03)*

The support of the site leader was generally considered one of the most integral dimensions of support for staff in their work. *"The [site leader] is very supportive and so is everyone else" (INT 13)*. A number of educators also mentioned the support they experienced from young people. This support was evident when staff witnessed the growth and change apparent in the lives of young people. *"I think it's actually good to be able to see a growth within the young people as well" (INT 07)*. Support from young people was also evident through the genuine and reciprocal care and concern offered by young people in authentic relationships with educators, and by the openness of young people to engage in programs guided by the operation by principles model incorporating respect, participation, safe and legal, and honesty.

> *But the young people are actually the ones that are the biggest [support]. I find that, sometimes I'll go in and feel like I'll doubt my ability and then I walk into school and the young people help me recognise that. (INT 15)*

Critical reflection for self-awareness and awareness of others:

Local site support

- *How does your local site leader offer support to staff?*
- *What support strategies are in place for educators at your local flexi school?*

- *When things are not going well for your team, how do you access wider support than what is available at your local site?*
- *Are you aware of the support offered to your site leader? What support are you able to offer to your site leader?*
- *Does your team generally feel supported by each other?*
- *What practical strategies could you initiate or suggest for your team to experience higher levels of support from colleagues?*

Reflection and Supervision

Some staff mentioned the support they experienced through reflection for self-awareness and professional supervision. Reflective practice and supervision was offered internally by the organisation through access to a professional counsellor or at times with the local site leader.

> *And having regular supervision I found was, with um, just with [site leader], and also when I first started, with a [more experienced worker] as well. I found [supervision] essential and really great for anyone and particularly for any new practitioner. (INT 06)*

One educator talked about external supervision and recognised the value of this kind of support in their professional work.

> *I think I would explain [supervision] as a support mechanism, it's a support mechanism in so far as it's an external support mechanism, where you can actually be supported by another person um, that's not anything to do with staff and I think that's important - a bit of distance. I think a bit of distance is actually very important. It makes sense. (INT 07)*

Some sites arranged regular group supervision or reflective practice as another mechanism of support for staff in their work. Reflective practice and supervision was valued by those who had participated in the sessions.

> *[Having] enough space to talk about why, why do you do it like that? Why do you do this? What would you do in this situation? So I guess a lot of time for reflecting on how things are done and why things are done that way. Where that idea comes from … so there's a lot of time for discussion and reflection, these are really important, because I don't know that they're – it's not like you can go off somewhere else where you can find out how to do it – you really have to do this. (INT 03)*

Ann Morgan, Ph.D.

Critical reflection for self-awareness and awareness of others:

Reflection and supervision

- *What has been your experience of reflective practice and supervision at your local site? How could you learn more?*
- *If you are unclear about the purpose of reflective practice, who could you discuss this with in your team or beyond?*
- *What are the blocks that you experience personally, or within your team, regarding finding time and space to reflect on practice or engage in supervision conversations?*

Flexible and Honest Ways of Working

The next common thread identified in the data related to staff support was *flexible and honest ways of working*. This flexibility and honesty was apparent when staff felt able to admit when they were struggling with an aspect of their work or with a particular young person.

> *I think one of the areas that is very difficult in this is you feel isolated or you can feel isolated, you can feel you're the only one having troubles, but that's certainly not true. You're really the only person not having trouble (laugh), if you believe that you're not having trouble. And I think that's what comes out in these conversations and I've gone down to [school site] and different times when people are sort of ah, a bit cagey about what they're talking about and I basically say, "you know it is OK to be struggling with this" and they go "Oh God, I thought I was the only one". And I say, "look I've had all this experience and I'm struggling", um so, you know, so I think they relax a little bit more when they can hear that people [struggle]. (INT 05)*

Flexibility and honesty was evident through the collegiality and equality experienced in working relationships with other staff where individuals felt they were working in a flexible and honest way. *"You're really working in partnership and you're working as equals and it's about negotiation and compromise and listening" (INT 09).* This teacher identified that her experience of working in the network was a *"backflip from the authority model of being teacher" (INT 09)* that had been experienced in another conventional education setting. Flexibility was also experienced by staff when they felt encouraged to run with new ideas and try new things. A staff member commented that working with people in flexi schools allowed a greater freedom of information sharing and a greater flexibility.

Critical reflection for self-awareness and awareness of others:

Flexible and honest ways of working

- *In your staff team, what do you do to foster connections (within and beyond your flexi school)?*
- *How do you encourage and support your colleagues to be honest about the challenges they face in their practice?*
- *How do you support staff to find the strengths in what they already know and what they can already do?*
- *How flexible are you to try a new or different approach in your practice? Are you open and willing to learn from your colleagues?*

Seeing the Bigger Picture

The final common thread identified in the data for *staff support* was *seeing the bigger picture*. This thread was expressed in a range of ways and in a variety of spheres. At a personal level, for some staff, seeing the bigger picture was connected to their own sense of spirituality and purpose in their work as educators. This perspective was expressed by two educators in the following ways:

> *I do have a strong sense of being part of a bigger picture and in all honesty I have a big sense of support from the spirit. The spirit and all that kind of thing and in all honesty I pray every day before I go in every day and I sort of pray when I come out and it's not really religious but it's a calling in of whatever I can be. That actually is a massive support. (INT 15)*
>
> *I feel that what I do, I'm not just going to a job, you know, that it has a purpose. And what I like about here, people don't realise it, a lot that kids don't realise that the Christian Brothers are doing ministry here that's cutting edge, all these kids realise is that no one gets expelled, what they're getting here is unconditional love and that constant forgiveness. They don't know that, 'cause out in the world it's three strikes and you're gone, OK? (INT 13)*

For other staff, seeing the bigger picture influenced the way they viewed their work as educators on a day to day level. This was captured when staff recognised that education was broader than curriculum and that in their work of enfranchising young people, relationships were always the first priority. At a wider organisational level, seeing the bigger picture entailed staff having awareness that they were part of a network of schools beyond their local site and that they could access support and resources through this wider network.

> *I think the (network) is, it's a godsend. It's a whole network of youth workers, teachers, [support staff], coordinators – everyone supports one another. You only need to say the word. I'm having problems in this area or, you know for everyone to give you as much support as you need. (INT 08)*

Beyond the organisation, seeing the bigger picture included networking with those in the local community and with relevant agencies such as those in the youth work sector.

> *I guess I do a lot of sort of networking stuff, so I'll, like in the past I've worked for things with [other agency] . . . and get some funding for that, and talking it through with them and building up the ideas around training and get some for funding around that ... I'm on a couple of reference groups – one's about [the youth work] sector ... so what sort of support and development for youth workers. And I'll go on another one about engaging, how to engage young people who are disengaging, from education. (INT 03)*

In a political and ideological sense, seeing the bigger picture involved offering a challenge to the very notion of what education entailed and how it can be enacted. One educator eloquently articulated that the practice of education experienced in the network context offered a unique and important perspective contributing to the wider social discourse of education.

> *I think these places offer a model of excellence around what pedagogy and what learning can be like. I'm really glad that the best of educators, the people who choose to work with us, all show the commitment to reflect and delve into themselves, and to challenge themselves, and at the same time, want to work with this disadvantaged group of young people. I think these places actually offer and stand in front of a fair bit of what can be seen in the current economic climate, as being a revisionist kind of approach to education. And in that sense, the very existence of these places becomes radical. Places like this need to exist to challenge other systems, so in that kind of hegemonic sense, they are extremely important as a political and pedagogic point of difference. (INT 16)*

Critical Reflection for self-awareness and awareness of others:

Seeing the bigger picture

- *How has your broad view of the nature and purpose of education been formed?*
- *What has influenced your capacity to see the importance of the work you do at a local level in relation to a broader perspective on the nature and purpose of education?*
- *Who has inspired you in terms of your own philosophy of education?*
- *When does your team take time to discuss these 'bigger picture' notions of education?*
- *What are the blocks at an individual and local site level that get in the way of engaging in this dialogue?*

PART III

Models to Support Relational Practice

6

Relational Dynamics

A Sociocultural Model of Identity and Development in Practice

Educator identity and development in practice in flexi schools involves an interplay between particular ways of working and ways of professional learning. These ways of being and becoming educator are expressed through social relationships in social practices. Social practices are the ways people interact and relate that become part of the normal fabric of everyday life. For example, a social practice in flexi schools is working within the operation by principles model or having morning meetings in which young people's voices are valued and listened to. In order to capture the dynamic interplay that exists in practice between ways of working and ways of professional learning, a sociocultural model called *relational dynamics* was developed through my research (see figure 13).

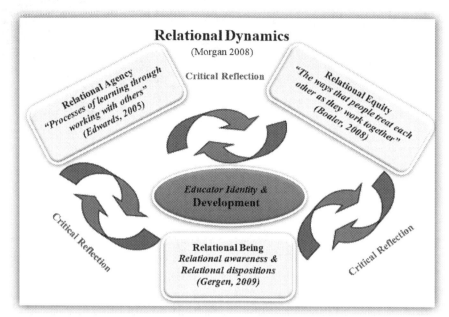

Figure 13. Relational dynamics – a sociocultural model of identity and development in multidisciplinary communities of practice.

Three key elements of this model are: *relational agency; relational equity;* and *relational being.* These elements can be enacted more intentionally when supported by *critical reflection.* Each element of the model of *relational dynamics* will now be explained.

Relational Agency — The First Element of *Relational Dynamics*

Relational agency is particularly relevant for multidisciplinary practice — a key feature of practice in flexi schools. This was evident in research on alternative education identified in my literature review (refer to Appendix B for a summary of themed groups of features of best practice in alternative education). Relational agency involves the process of learning through working with others to interpret and respond to challenges in practice. It involves skills such as the capacity to: collaborate; work across professional boundaries; cooperate; include diverse perspectives; draw on diverse experience; act for improved outcomes; offer support and ask for support; work with difference;

influence and be influenced by others (Edwards, 2005) For an illustration of this element see figure 14 below.

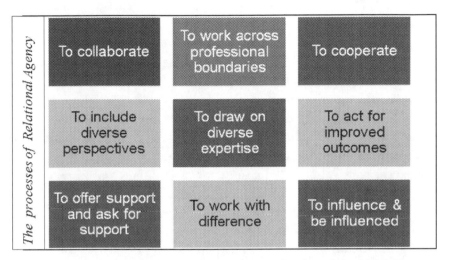

Figure 14. The processes of relational agency. Learning through working with others (Edwards. 2005).

Developing relational agency enhances the capacity of educators to learn from the difficulties and challenges of their practice through collaboration and the sharing of issues with other educators — especially those from other professional backgrounds. Relational agency can expand educators' understanding of challenging issues to allow expertise to be responsively expressed in actions. Through exercising relational agency, responsive professional identities are formed (Edwards, 2005). In my research on educator identity and development in flexi schools, relational agency was evident when staff gave primacy to relationships with young people. It was evident when productive relationships with colleagues were seen as essential in terms of achieving better outcomes for young people. Relational agency within flexi schools was particularly evident when teachers described the importance they placed on learning from young people and from youth workers, social workers or counsellors. It was also apparent when educators described the importance of working closely with Aboriginal and Torres Strait Islander educators whose cultural capital and expertise was vital in terms of learning to re-engage young people in culturally appropriate ways.

Ann Morgan, Ph.D.

Relational Equity – The Second Element of *Relational Dynamics*

The second element of the model of *Relational Dynamics* was *relational equity* (Boaler, 2008). Relational equity makes explicit values-based practices such as the ways that people treat each other as they work together (Boaler, 2008). Ways of working that are socially inclusive and equitable, based on ethics derived from human rights principles and notions of participatory democracy align with the values that underpin practice in the flexi schools. These underpinning values include not only working with the four principles of respect, participation, safe and legal, and honesty, but also the values of caring and community. These values shape how educators negotiate and co-construct their identity with young people. The values underpinning practice were expressed through social interactions characterised by equitable ways of working that included: valuing diversity; valuing active listening; giving voice to all; acting in equitable ways; valuing genuine curiosity; respecting others; enacting care for others; valuing different perspectives; and having concern for the common good (see figure 15 below). These ways of working in educational settings are needed for life and work in the 21ˢᵗ Century.

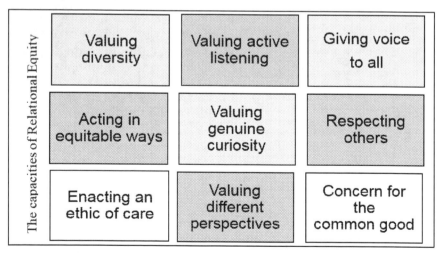

Figure 15. The capacities of relational equity: The ways people should treat each other as they work together (Boaler, 2008).

When considering education for the 21st Century and the impact of contemporary economic, social and cultural shifts requiring new ways of understanding and providing education (Wyn, 2008), a framework of education from the United Nations Educational, Scientific and Cultural Organization (UNESCO), also has relevance for the flexi schools' context (Delors, 1999). The four pillars of education for the 21st Century, "learning to know, learning to do, learning to be, and learning to live together"(Delors, 1999, p. 14) resonates with the model of education in flexi schools that was described by educators.

I considered this framework through a relational lens when applied to the flexi schools. For example, educators experienced "learning to know" and "learning to do", through participation in social relationships. Through working with others, especially those from other professional backgrounds, educators learnt how to "know" and "do". Their broadened interpretations of challenging aspects of practice (learning to know), and their increased options for action (learning to do) were developed as they exercised relational agency. "Learning to live together" was experienced in the flexi schools as people engaged with the four principles, enacted caring relationships and fostered a sense of inclusive community that supported relationships in an ongoing way. "Learning to live together" was experienced when relationships were given primacy, when educators were willing to change their perspectives through critical reflection and when they were able to increase their capacity to hold complexity. "The art of holding complexity is the ability to face conflict and other life challenges through collaboration, self-awareness and flexibility rather than through control and coercion" (Morgan et al., 2014, p.579). "Learning to live together" is clearly aligned with relational equity, which is reflected in the quality of relationships in the learning community.

Relational Being — The Third Element of *Relational Dynamics*

The third element of *relational dynamics — relational being —* is most close in meaning to the pillar of "learning to be" from the framework of education for the 21st Century. In the research interviews, educators discussed their experiences of enacting, observing, and living out certain dispositions in their relationships with young people and with colleagues. Dispositions captured the interconnectedness of all aspects of relationships in flexi schools. The idea of relational being was coined by Gergen (2009), who describes it as a movement from viewing the self as a separate entity, an individual bounded being, towards viewing and understanding the self as constituted in relationships. In many ways it is similar to the African concept of Ubuntu that was mentioned by an educator who was interviewed in my study. Although we do not have a similar word in English, Ubuntu (Flippin, 2012) is described as follows:

> *The philosophy of Ubuntu derives from a Nguni word, ubuntu meaning "the quality of being human." Ubuntu manifests itself through various human acts, clearly visible in social, political, and economic situations, as well as among family. According to sociolinguist Buntu Mfenyana, it "runs through the veins of all Africans, is embodied in the oft-repeated: "Ubuntu ngumtu ngabanye abantu" ("A person is a person through other people").*
>
> *This African proverb reveals a world view that we owe our selfhood to others, that we are first and foremost social beings, that, if you will, no man/woman is an island, or as the African would have it, "One finger cannot pick up a grain." Ubuntu is, at the same time, a deeply personal philosophy that calls on us to mirror our humanity for each other. To the observer, ubuntu can be seen and felt in the spirit of willing participation, unquestioning cooperation, warmth, openness, and personal dignity demonstrated by the indigenous black population. From the cradle, every black child inculcates these qualities so that by the time adulthood is reached, the ubuntu philosophy has become a way of being.*

Relational being is evident in educational trends that privilege relationships (Bingham & Sidorkin, 2004; Noddings, 1992; Sidorkin, 2000; Smyth, 2006; Vadeboncoeur & Vellos, 2016). It is expressed in educational trends that are participatory and democratic (Apple & Beane, 2007; Ayers, 2009; Dewey, 2010). In education that supports and appreciates the dignity of every human being (Freire, 2000; Noddings, 1992), and is inclusive of difference (Lederach, 2005; UNESCO, 1994), relational being is manifest. These ideas reflect an observable trend in contemporary human thinking regarding how we understand "identity" and "the self".

This shift in understanding is also apparent in the field of science through the work of physicists, biologists, and environmentalists and in the ideas of those who are systems thinkers and complexity theorists (Capra, 1975, 1997, 2004; de Chardin, 1959; Suzuki, McConnell & Mason, 2007). Interconnectedness of life and relationships is a significant feature of Indigenous knowledge and worldviews (Gair, Miles & Thomson, 2005; Knudston & Suzuki, 1992; Matthews, Watego, Cooper & Baturo, 2005; Sheehan & Walker, 2001). A shift towards the interconnectedness of relational ways of being is evident among some leaders and innovators in the business world (Covey, 2011; Holman, 2010; Holman et al., 2007; Owen, 2008; Scharmer, 2008; Senge, 2006; Senge, Scharmer, Jaworski & Flowers, 2004; Wheatley, 2006). It is evident in social psychology (Gergen, 2009), psychiatry and interpersonal and relational neurobiology (Perry, 2009; Siegel, 2006). Philosophies and spiritualities that emphasise non-violence and non-dualistic thinking also reflect this shift towards interconnectedness and relational ways of being (Berry, 2006; de Chardin, 1959; Lederach, 2005; Macy & Johnstone, 2012).

The Centrality of Relationships and Interconnectedness

The common thread emerging in these diverse disciplines and fields of learning and practice is the idea that relationships and interconnectedness are central, defining aspects of life, influencing ways of being in relationship with self, others, earth, and life force — inclusive of the many and varied ways "life force" may be defined. This relational view of being has implications for the practice of educators in flexi schools. The initial purpose of developing the model of *relational dynamics* was to see if it was relevant to educators in flexi schools. Educators described how their ways of being in relationships enhanced their capacity to work more effectively with young people and staff, supporting their capacity to enact relational agency and relational equity. Relational being matters because of the strength of educators' perceptions of their relational dispositions evident in the data. These are

relationship with others is a central element of a broader, integrated notion of human functioning. Human functioning can be expressed internally in the thinking mind or through emotional, physical, spiritual and social dimensions. All expressions of human functioning — including mental, physical, emotional, spiritual, and social functioning — have the capacity to support learning and development. Human functioning is mediated in and through relationships and cultural tools or mediational means. For example, through language and other cultural symbols, including art, music, and activities that emphasise physical, sensory and emotional ways of being. Relationships may be physically present or embodied in the memory and identity of an individual, but they are nonetheless present in some way.

The limitation of an education system still deeply entrenched in an understanding of learning predominantly defined as cognitive processes in an academic sense, confined to an individual bounded self, needs to be challenged and expanded. Such limitations are heightened for those who have experienced multiple complexities in their lives including social exclusion from conventional schooling. The struggle to appreciate the breadth and potential of all levels of human functioning and its capacity to support learning is a limitation of a system operating from paradigms that are no longer constructive for the health, wellbeing and inclusion of all (Wyn, 2008). The current system is no longer an appropriate model of education for the 21st Century (Delors, 1999; FYA, 2017).

Relational being increases the capacity for people to exercise agency as they negotiate and co-create their identities and learning capacities through a wide range of human functions. If the potential agency to act on the world enabled through identity formation in relationship was recognised, the significance of relationships in learning could be further explored and intentionally privileged in conventional education settings. The repertoires of identity performance or relational being and becoming are multiple (Gergen, 2009). This widening of relational repertoires for identity formation was exemplified as staff and young people in the flexi schools found safety to negotiate their identities in more flexible ways than what they had experienced in more traditional contexts. The potential for creative innovation was broadened. Various shifts and movements in educator identity and development in practice were made possible in the context through the emphasis on relationships, reflection and holding complexity. Identity formation, as an experience of learning and development, embedded in interconnected relationships with young people and other staff, provided access to a wider repertoire of ways of being an educator. This repertoire contrasts with the more limited options for being an educator that are available when identity is construed from an individualist perspective, understood within notions of a bounded self (Gergen, 2009), and limited to a narrow conceptualisation of cognitive processes.

Critical Reflection — The Final Element of *Relational Dynamics*

Educators in this study perceived the importance of being reflective and self-aware in their practice. Findings from data analysis indicate that practitioners appreciate that reflective practice significantly influences them as they negotiate and co-create their sense of identity and development. This enables them to make observable shifts in their educator identity in practice. When educators are willing to engage in critical reflection in and on practice, these reflective processes act like catalysts for developing relational agency, relational equity and a greater sense of relational being. For this reason, critical reflection is included in the model of *relational dynamics*. The dynamic interplay between the three main components of the relational dynamics model — relational agency, relational equity and relational being — is animated and enacted through critical reflection (Morgan, 2017). As educators intentionally engage in critical self-reflection, unconscious patterns of behaviour in relationships with young people and colleagues can be made conscious and explicit. Educators who are willing to become more self-aware, are generally able to engage more responsively with young people and colleagues. Through understanding and enacting the relational dynamics model, reactive and punitive engagement with young people can be minimised and transformed.

Critical reflection in flexi schools was strengthened through the influence of educators who are aware of the significance of engaging in regular reflective practice. Some educators in the flexi schools with a teaching background were influenced by their colleagues with a community services background, to shift towards a commitment to engage more actively in critical reflection. As educators developed greater self-awareness around the influence of values, beliefs, emotions and assumptions regarding the nature of education and the nature of learners, change was possible. Without conscious awareness, educators can fall into the trap of applying stereotypes and labels to young people. Unconscious bias may show up in a lack of understanding of the complex issues young people face. Rather than reactive and blaming approaches, young people need informed and responsive approaches.

Critical reflection supports educators in the flexi schools' context to enact relational equity. As educators face challenging issues in practice, some accept the invitation to interrogate their own assumptions and reactions in different situations. They carefully consider how these assumptions and reactions interact with and affect their practice. This engagement in critical reflection becomes the starting point for conversation, dialogue, negotiation and co-construction of educator identity and development in practice. Educators who are open to engaging in processes of dialogue with other staff and with young people, who value diversity, and who are open to be inclusive of difference, seem to be more able to hold complexity in the midst of their work with young people.

The Significance of Young People in *Relational Dynamics*

The repertoires of identity performance for educators in the flexi schools extend as they engage with the particular group of young people who exercise agency and make choices to re-engage in these learning communities. The agency of young people, which at times includes their resilience and their resistance (Alpert, 1991; Thompson, Entwisle, Alexander & Sundius, 1992), challenges educators in the flexi schools to find other ways of working that are more inclusive and democratic. These other ways of working are supported by using the four principles of respect, participation, safe and legal, and honesty. The four principles provide a framework for educators and young people to enter into dialogue, to listen to understand, and to adopt a strengths-based perspective. The operation by principles model provides relational space for young people to have a voice and make choices in the context of a relationship focussed community. This way of working requires educators to navigate their professional identities in different ways than what they may have experienced in conventional education settings.

For young people as well, opportunities to redefine their identity as learners occur through mutually respectful relationships with adults and peers within the learning community. A young person's learning identity that may have been fractured through frequent experiences of failure and exclusion, through being blamed and viewed as the source of the problem of non-completion of school, can be re-negotiated within a learning community that adopts and embodies the operation by principles model — a relationship focussed way of being and working. Using the four principles shifts the emphasis from the individual as learner, or the individual as teacher, to an individual person constituted in the first instance as a relational being, interconnected through relationships within a community.

The four principles call people to accountability within the learning community. The overemphasis on individualism in our culture (Ageyev, 2003; Bingham, 2004; Gergen, 2009) requires shifting. Emphasising relational ways of being and operating through principles, enables a relational perspective on resilience to be adopted (Vadeboncoeur, 2012). Adults and young people engage in processes of 'place making' (Vadeboncoeur, 2012) by creating and strengthening relational and symbolic-spatial connections of meaning and identity. These relational and place making processes support young people to exercise agency through meaning making in relationships, located in place. Educators offer young people practical support to grow and develop in and through relationships over time. Meaning making processes, such as making connections to place, in and through relationships, enhances young people's ability to exercise and develop agency in their lives and in their worlds. They develop resilience through interconnected relationships.

Relational Perspectives and the Four Principles

Engaging with the four principles emphasises a relational perspective on communication in education. This occurs through shared meaning making in conversation and dialogue (Biesta, 2004). Enacting the four principles and understanding that they apply equally to young people and adults enables a more relational perspective on authority and power in education to be considered and experienced (Bingham,

2004). Similarly, adopting a relational perspective on learning makes caring relationships possible (Thayer-Bacon, 2004) and young person-centred learning a priority.

Relational perspectives on curriculum design and pedagogy (Bingham & Sidorkin, 2004), that incorporate the enactment of the four principles, support the development of a young person's learning trajectory, inclusive of them having a voice and being able to make choices. This relational perspective on learning supports the lived experience of democracy, rather than merely limiting the experience of democracy to learning about democracy. In all of these ways and in many others that are not captured here, relational perspectives embodying the four principles, inform and influence the formation of educator identities of adults; identities that are negotiated in and through relational ways of being in the context of flexi school communities.

The Formation and Development of Educator Identities

In these educational sites — these educating communities of practice — the formation and development of educator identities occurs in many intersecting spaces. Adults and young people alike are both teachers and learners. The distance between a learner and a more experienced other may be changed or bridged through a range of relational strategies for being and becoming, for experiencing and learning (Vygotsky, 1978). For example, learning may include a breadth of experiences including direct instruction, and move through, across, or around the spectrum of learning strategies to other practices of experiential learning or learning through dialogue and negotiation (Renshaw, 2004).

In the flexi schools learning and development occur in embodied places of relationship for educators and young people alike. Depending on the situation and the needs of the learner, educators and young people can enact a wide range of strategies as they rehearse, perform, adopt, explore, and experiment with, the different parts of their learner and educator identities. The experience of an educator, the supportive relationships within the community, and the voices of relationship that have shaped each person's life (Bakhtin, 1981), create a place for relational ways of being to be negotiated.

The emphasis on relationships and flexibility within the learning place create a wide range of opportunities to explore identity formation and to create new possibilities of being and becoming. The agency of each adult and young person enables them, if they choose, to engage in various degrees of negotiation, in order to co-create different ways of being an educator and of being a learner. This process is captured by Gergen (2009, p.275), who states:

> *Thus the best option is flexibility. Drawing from one's resources as a multi-being, one should be readied to access many different voices, to move fluidly with the shifting tides of dialogue . . . one should be able to engage in collaborative dialogue in one situation, serve as a mentor in another, or variously act as a facilitator, an agent of empowerment or a friend. The move towards richer relationships is not intended to obliterate the traditional role of monologic knower and disciplinarian. It is not that the traditional relationship is bankrupt; it is simply limited.*

Part of my motivation for writing this series of books was to explore how the application and experiences of *relational dynamics*, including relational agency, relational equity, relational being and critical reflection, influence educator identity and development in local flexi school sites. This could be another area for further research. How these relational ways of being influence the identity and development of young people as learners, in particular how young people's learner identities are co-constructed and re-formed in social relationships, also has potential for further research.

Additionally, the exploration of different ways of being an educator through the examination of ways of working and ways of professional learning that are negotiated within the social contexts of flexi schools may highlight the potential for enhanced agency as educators develop an understanding of *relational dynamics*. An understanding of the dynamic interplay between relational agency, relational equity, relational being and critical reflection, as outlined in the model of *relational dynamics*, could be further developed through professional learning. This has the potential to contribute to the capacity of an individual in the process of being and becoming an educator in flexi schools to enfranchise young people. It may inform educators in other settings who find themselves working with young people who are at-risk of disengaging. Further research on these areas would be beneficial for educators working with this cohort of young people. The ways in which *relational dynamics* could be applied in a wider range of educational and other multidisciplinary settings also holds potential for further research.

My research has highlighted the importance of staff induction and professional learning that is situated in practice, and that supports the development of a growing appreciation of the significance of relationships, reflection and the ability to hold complexity in ways of working. Through engaging in Reflective Practice Groups in local contexts, some staff appeared to develop greater capacity to be critically reflective and open to shift towards different ways of being an educator in the flexi schools. Further exploration of how to continue to embed critical reflection into everyday work practice; particularly for new staff in their induction period, may become apparent over time.

Another implication of this research for practice in the flexi schools would be to consider the development of staff mentoring processes that emphasise *relational dynamics,* the interplay of relational agency, relational equity, relational being and critical reflection. This could be further explored through developing professional learning that promotes an appreciation of the importance of the four elements of the model of *relational dynamics.* These are linked with the three overarching themes of *relational practice, critical reflection* and *the art of holding complexity,* in ways of working and ways of professional learning.

7

Personal Dispositions for Relational Being

A range of personal qualities of educators were identified in the data analysis that enhanced relationships with young people and, which over time, supported more positive engagement and the provision of relevant and meaningful learning opportunities. Some of these qualities include wisdom, patience, humour, acceptance of where young people are at, being young at heart, being sensitive, caring, tolerant, compassionate and empathetic. These qualities or dispositions are enacted in different ways, yet appear to support the development of relational capacity in adults. The influence of the flexi schools' context on educator identity and development in practice is evident in that educators are able to invest time in developing personal capacities and skills that have a relational focus. For those who struggle with this aspect of practice, achieving positive outcomes with young people is often more problematic.

Dispositions are described by Diez (2007) as something that matures in an incremental way "developing over time . . . influenced by context, experience and interaction" (p. 390). Diez highlights that an integrated approach does not view dispositions as part of a fixed entity or feature of character in a moral sense. The development of dispositions is closely connected to the context of practice. Developing various dispositions is enhanced through critical reflection on practice.

A cautionary word

No educator can adopt positive dispositions in every situation on every day. While being aware of what relational dispositions may look like in practice, it is equally important to understand and become aware of those times when they are not being enacted in relationships by ourselves and others. Of greater importance than getting it right every time is being able to ask the challenging questions regarding what needs to happen next, for example:

- *How do we give ourselves room and space to grow into being a relational practitioner?*
- *When under pressure, what is the default position that I adopt?*
- *How can this be transformed and changed within myself?*
- *When it all goes wrong, how do I make improvements?*
- *How do I reconnect with young people and colleagues following conflict?*
- *How do I access support when I am reactive to young people rather than responsive?*
- *Do I understand the factors that are influencing my reactions? e.g. are my reactions linked to my values, beliefs and assumptions?*
- *How can I learn to make new choices in new circumstances?*

These questions are the basis of the work of critical reflection which is the focus of the second book in this series. Obviously each of the overarching themes, including *relational practice*, are interconnected and weave throughout all elements of practice.

Examples of Dispositions Evident in Educator Responses

Examples of certain dispositions or ways of being that were highlighted by educators in interviews are outlined in this section of the book. Educators described certain ways of being in relationship with young people and colleagues as they discussed their practice. My role as researcher was to synthesise what was said by educators in 16 interviews. To provide greater authenticity and reliability in analysis, I collaborated with another researcher, who also coded the responses.

We subsequently met and together arrived at categories of dispositions drawn from educators' responses (see Appendix C for a list of relational dispositions).

The majority of all disposition statements were interpersonal in nature. Relationships were supported by interpersonal dispositions such as *"being authentic in relationships"*, *"being respectful and gentle"*, and *"being safe to express yourself"*. Interpersonal disposition statements also included *"being able to apply the four principles to self and others"* and *"being willing to build genuine relationships"*. The number of dispositions connected to developing positive and healthy interpersonal relationships far exceeded the other dispositions related to personal and organisational capacity.

Being able to embody the principles

When staff talked about the principles as *"a living breathing"* entity they were describing the embodiment of the principles. Embodying the principles included being authentic in living the principles and therefore being a role model for the young people. One person felt that embodying the principles was like *"being a beacon to young people" (INT 05)* in terms of role-modelling to them how to live by those values.

Applying the same values to themselves that were applied to the young people was also an expression of embodying the principles. If young people could not consume alcohol on site, one educator felt that adults also needed to take that on board, even after hours. Another staff member captured the idea of embodying the four principles when he talked about how the young people *"learn more from what we do, not from what we say" (INT 02)*. By being accountable to the principles as much as the young people were, another educator felt a responsibility to hold himself accountable to the community through the principles. A number of educators highlighted that the principles were for everybody, not just for young people.

This sense of collective responsibility linked the four principles back into a real community of people — not merely an abstract concept but a lived reality. Embracing the principles in the whole of life was a way of embodying *"the key principles that we live on a day to day basis as humans" (INT 08)*, such as respecting one another and respecting yourself. Being respectful was identified as a central value within the flexi schools' context.

It was evident to a number of educators that young people could clearly *"identify someone who acts on the principles" (INT 02)* in all aspects of life as an embodied experience. When another educator talked about the principles he recognised that his own enacting and embodiment of the principles was an encouragement and model for young people and colleagues to be willing to take risks and have a go, especially in terms of participation and honesty. It was clear that some staff recognised the value of the principles as a foundation for everything and whilst appreciating that it was hard to *"genuinely internalise them" (INT 15),* it was perceived as essential in this work. Embodying the principles included learning to resolve conflict non-violently and to recognise democracy and equity in their operation. This was expressed in terms of genuinely listening to young people and ensuring that *"everyone having a say" (INT 14)* was a lived reality within the school community.

Being respectful

Many staff talked about being respectful, which included being respectful of self, respectful of one another and being respectful of the circumstances in young people's lives. It involved adults *"respecting the dignity of each person" (INT 01),* and ensuring that this was the basis of all relationships. Respect was seen as an important focus in the work with young people as it was the starting point and launching pad for enacting other principles. When coupled with gentleness and an appreciation that everyone had experienced something in their lives that had not worked for them, it was felt that respect made sense to young people.

The disposition of being respectful towards young people supported staff to work with young people in a manner that was not reliant on *"managing behaviour"* or using strategies to control the group. Being respectful was not just being *"nice"* and *"weak"* it was about *"being firm and caring" (INT 14).* In addition to this, another educator saw the importance of being respectful of the circumstances in young people's lives and extending towards them a sense of unconditional love (INT 15). For another educator, being respectful was associated with *"loving the unlovable, to treat people with the same respect that you want to be treated with yourself" (INT 05)*. Enacting respect demonstrated a capacity or disposition to engage with others in the moment for a particular purpose. This is challenging when it is sometimes easier to let things slip, to not have that follow up conversation with a young person or colleague.

For another educator, the building of relationships through being respectful was the starting point for experiencing trust in staff relationships. One educator described her experience of being respected by her peers in the learning community as an example of the respect commonly extended to the young people. Such a disposition of respect enacted by her peers and colleagues enabled her to be fully herself (INT 14).

Being safe

Safety was understood holistically in terms of being *"emotionally, spiritually, physically, and intellectually safe" (INT 16)* and this kind of safety was described as the essence of these school communities. This level of safety was important for everyone, both young people and staff. Being safe was also linked to the freedom to have a voice, to say your own piece and *"to be safe to express yourself in the way you want to express yourself" (INT 16)*. Being safe was identified as a basic human need. When discussing the disposition of safety, educators talked about being safe enough to be able to take a risk — have a go — in the same way that they were hoping young people would feel safe to have a go (INT 12). Being safe was associated with being legal because your actions affected everyone.

Being honest

Staff talked about being honest in terms of the capacity to be honest about *"not knowing everything"* and being honest with sharing personal stories and *"being true to yourself" (INT 05)*. This kind of honesty required a disposition of being open.

121

Being open

Being open was frequently mentioned in terms of *"being open to admit mistakes"*, *"being open and honest if things were not working"*, and *"being willing to make amends through apologising when necessary" (INT 01)*. This kind of openness enabled people to learn from mistakes and required being open-minded and open in attitude. The disposition of being open was sustained by an acknowledgement of the need to be open and willing to seek assistance when you as an educator were uncertain or unsure.

The challenge in staff relationships to remain open and honest about one's struggles, limitations, and needing help or support in the work with young people, was acknowledged by another educator. Building those kinds of honest and supportive relationships amongst colleagues took time and required trust and being able to recognise storytelling as opening up to others (INT 05). While educators would often encourage young people to being open in this way, it was sometimes perceived as more difficult for staff, particularly new staff, to be open with their peers and colleagues about such things as *"not knowing"* or *"needing help" (INT 01)*. For those educators who were able to adopt these dispositions of openness, the experience of *"becoming more capable" (INT 09)* over time, through support and mentoring from other staff, was not uncommon.

When talking about adult to adult relationships in the workplace, another participant stated that they had to *"be someone that was approachable, open, understands, sits down, talks the same language" (INT 12)* with colleagues. These dispositions or relational capacities to engage were perceived to be just as important between colleagues as they were with young people. Being open in these ways were valued by this educator and another colleague who both recognised that it came from the emphasis on relationships with all people in the learning community.

One educator talked about being available and open to learn from listening, and to learn from young people and their families and *"what they're looking for" (INT 16)*. Being able to listen to young people was an expression of being open to learn from the young people rather than always being in the position of "teacher" and this was challenging for some staff. Traditional notions of what it means to be a teacher, conjure authoritarianism and needing to be the expert (Alsup, 2006; Britzman, 2003). These authoritarian ways of being an educator are changed over time in this context. When educators deliberately choose to adopt the disposition of becoming a co-learner with young people they challenge authoritarian models.

In discussing relationships with young people, another educator mentioned staff responsibility to make some sort of helpful relationship with young people which required being open *"by being a little bit vulnerable" (INT 07)*. This disposition of openness required a sensitivity to where young people were coming from *"and what they've got to offer as well" (INT 07)*. Dispositions of being open-minded with young people and being open in attitude were further examples of dispositions that supported relational ways of working with young people. Additionally, educators made reference to being open and honest with feelings and being able to discuss emotional upsets (INT 01). Such openness can be an expression of caring for others and demonstrates an appreciation of the importance of emotional intelligence, fostered through prioritising relationships first.

Being relational

Being able to recognise the primary importance of relationships was a disposition highlighted by a number of staff. This disposition was evident when staff were able to see curriculum as secondary to relationships and when they were willing to build genuine relationships with young people. One educator stated that *"the content of the curriculum isn't all that significantly important in the young people's lives at the moment and that education is much broader than As, Bs or Cs" (INT 05)*.

Being able to engage with and maintain genuine relationships and connection with others required being present to others and genuinely interested in their wellbeing. In order to sustain these relational dispositions staff also need to be able to recognise the difficulties of relationships for young people due to the complexities in their lives. Staff had to be patient, accepting and understanding in relationships with young people and this required a relational disposition of being available and accessible to young people. At times a relational disposition required being challenging and compassionate in genuine relationships with young people.

Being committed

Being committed was perceived as important by a number of educators who recognised that the young people needed to have staff who were able to make a commitment to them and to their needs (INT 07). The commitment to this way of working involved: working with the four principles; reflecting on practice and on personal issues that may affect one's capacity to authentically engage with young people; and a commitment to critically reflect and challenge oneself and be open to change. Being accountable to the school community was seen as a responsibility of staff and young people alike (INT 07). The disposition of being able to recognise personal responsibility as well as being able to recognise a collective or collaborative approach to responsibility were expressions of dispositions of commitment by staff. Finally, being able to recognise the importance of commitment and support in ongoing relationships with young people was identified as an important feature of this work.

Being generous

Being able to recognise that generosity was evident in all different ways in the school community and being able to appreciate this generosity in all, were two relational dispositions described by educators in interviews.

Being caring and compassionate

Being caring was associated with being firm and being compassionate. The disposition of being caring was described by an educator when she talked about dealing with conflict amongst young people. She felt the approach adopted with young people at her school was a more caring approach than other contexts she had worked in and felt that caring included showing young people other ways of sorting out conflict (INT 14). She had heard a more experienced educator talk to young people reminding them of this.

*Look this is how we fix things here, you might go out and
there may be fights in your life. But maybe you remember, one
of the ways that you've learned to fix things differently here.
And we're trying to show you that there are other ways of doing
things. (INT 14)*

Being firm and caring was talked about in relation to using the
four principles as an alternative to other approaches of behaviour
management that tended to be more controlling. If being firm was
combined with being respectful and being human, it tended to result
in being fair as well as caring. Being caring was evident in the way
that young people were looked after by the staff. This was expressed
when young people were treated by adults with fairness, dignity and
respect. Being caring was associated with the idea of confronting and
challenging young people in a gentle way which may have involved
asking the young people:

*Why are you here? This is a practice run for real life. Here
you get feedback. In real life you might just get chucked out, yea?
I'm being fairly confrontational with that, but in a gentle way,
like they know I do it because I care. (INT 04)*

The disposition of being compassionate was also linked by one
educator to the idea of challenging young people *"to be the best young
person they could be" (INT 05)*. In this context, the challenge posed to
young people was about *"personal development"* and bringing *"a just
response in relationship with the young people, and you know, compassion
with young people" (INT 05)*.

Being hospitable

The disposition of hospitality included being welcoming. It was
related to the kind of treatment that people experienced when they
walked into the school, *"it doesn't matter if they're a young person, and
everyone gets the same kind of treatment" (INT 03)*. Being hospitable was
also about being present to people, *"hanging in with people"* in order to
maintain and sustain relationship, *"even when they're not coming" (INT
03)*. The disposition of hospitality required educators to be observant

and attentive to what was emerging in the practice context — *"I guess it's a lot of being around it to watch what happens and see how it goes. So I guess a lot of time for reflecting on how things are done and why things are done that way . . . so there's a lot of time for discussion and reflection"* (INT 03).

The disposition of hospitality incorporated inclusion. One educator talked about the importance of including young children as legitimate members of the school community when their parents were re-engaging in education. Building a community *"that people feel welcomed into and feel part of, I think that is significant to young people, they can be part of that"* (INT 07), was viewed as important. Being non-judgemental and non-biased were other aspects of being welcoming that contributed to the creation of a community of safety.

Being a role model

Being a role model to the young people was associated with the underlying values of the context and embodying the principles in terms of being loving and treating people with *"the same respect that you want to be treated yourself"* (INT 07). This capacity of role-modelling required a disposition of being able to recognise the influence of self on others and others on self, including young people. Being a role model was associated with being a co-learner with young people and this sentiment was captured by an educator who said that *"I feel I have as much to learn from the young people as they have to learn from me"* (INT 06). In a similar fashion being sensitive to others and what the young people have to offer was another way of role modelling a sense of mutuality and respect in relationships. Role models also needed to be able to recognise the strength in others, whether young people or colleagues. While mentoring was evident in relationships with young people it was also apparent between colleagues where more experienced educators were able to recognise the development of capacity in a less experienced colleague and support this through being patient (INT 09). In order for educators to experience being mentored by a role model in a positive way they needed to adopt a disposition of being able to learn through participation in doing and being, especially in relationship with others in the school community. *"[S]ucking in the importance I saw from people around me and learning and doing and just being"* (INT 10).

Being supportive and supported

Being supportive of others and being supported was perceived by staff as important in their ways of being in the flexi schools. When discussing staff support, participants indicated very strongly that they felt supported most often within their local context by their peers and particularly through their Head of Campus. In the interview data, the disposition of being supportive was expressed by one educator as a *"responsibility to help one another out" (INT 06)*. She experienced that support between staff within her school community and found that *"everyone is really supportive of each other" (INT 06)*. Similarly, another educator felt that the support offered by staff to each other was characteristic of the support commonly experienced within a family. This was echoed in a sentiment expressed by an educator who said that she had seen *"extraordinary acts of generosity and support when people [referring to other staff] have been in strife" (INT 10)*. At times it was perceived that support also included being able to recognise the confidence level in others and support the development of this to enable positive risk taking in the learning context and in relationships with young people. The dispositions of being supported by others and being supportive of others were experienced frequently by educators in this context. *"Just being supported and that's from top down, it's always there" (INT 11)*. Support from colleagues, and from the leader of the site was frequently experienced. *"Everyone's been really supportive, the [site leader] has been really supportive of my role" (INT 13)*.

For another person, the experience of being supportive in this context was about being able to work alongside others and that this was *"different to pretty much everywhere else I've worked. So I'm working alongside them and I'm there to support them, that's it" (INT 06)*. When discussing what was valued, another educator mentioned commitment and support. She felt that the commitment of the staff to the young people and to this way of working was valued. It included *"the relationships and the communication between one another and support . . . making sure people have access to that kind of support" (INT 09)*.

Another educator felt that staff appreciated *"the fact that everyone is treated respectfully"* and that this was a way of being supportive. Her perception was that *"no-one wants to be in an organisation where young people are treated unfairly or without much dignity or like numbers" (INT*

10). She valued *"the fact that there was no staff room gossip about young people or their parents" (INT 10),* highlighting that the disposition of being supportive through expressing generosity, care and respect was enacted and valued in her learning community. Some staff expressed the importance of experiencing support through being part of a unified staff team which was useful in then being able to support young people. Supporting young people required being able to recognise the tendency of young people to mask difficulties (INT 15). If this recognition was possible staff could more easily enact being supportive of young people's growth and development to be happy with themselves, *"with who they are and where they wanna go . . . to be there for them" (INT 08).*

Being authentic

The disposition of being authentic and genuine was recognised as significant especially in relationships with young people. It was discussed in terms of being authentic and consistent in living the four principles, acting on the principles, following the principles and internalising the principles. One educator talked about the importance of being able *"to enter into an authentic relationship with young people . . . around the boundaries of those principles" (INT 16).*

Being authentic was viewed as something young people could easily identify – *"someone from the heart, not someone from the head".* An educator commented that *"Our kids learn more from what we do, not from what we say. They learn from me, from who I am, the person first, rather than the Four Principles, then they get it" (INT 02).*

Being authentic was expressed as being able to be yourself because *"I get treated like a really valuable human being" (INT 14).* The disposition of being human was associated with *"respecting the dignity of each person"* and *"the humanity of everyone – the staff, the young people and the volunteers" (INT 01).* Being treated in this way enabled young people and staff to be able to recognise their own self-value and strengths. In this education context it was important for staff to develop the disposition of being able to recognise the balance between teaching and learning and the development of decency in each person. Another disposition that supported the fostering of this balance was being able to appreciate the value of humour and being playful or young at heart (INT 04).

Being understanding and patient

The disposition of being understanding of young people at a deep level was a feature of practice described by staff. Understanding young people at a deeper level than face value was a starting point for one educator. *"It's about understanding I think, and saying 'yea well I see where you're coming from, you know, it seems like you're getting back on your feet"* *(INT 11)*. The importance of being understanding was also relevant for staff relationships if they were based on honesty and trust.

Being understanding was linked with being patient. One educator appreciated that other staff were being patient in supporting her as she was learning how to do this work. Being patient and able to develop this patience was mentioned by another educator who talked about the patience between staff and the patience extended towards young people as aspects of the supportive environment within her particular school community. Another educator mentioned being patient and tolerant in relation to understanding the nature of the young people and *"why they are the way they are, which is the trauma and the effect of abuse" (INT 15)*. This person felt that the young people were equals and did not need her or need anything from her except being patient, being understanding and being accepting.

Being understanding and willing to take time with others, was an important disposition for relationships between staff and with young people. This was exemplified in the disposition of being trusting of others and demonstrating this trust in an ongoing way, which often required understanding and patience.

Being consistent

For one educator being consistent was described as *"being solid"* especially in relation to being unified as a staff team and working towards this unity in an ongoing way (INT 13). Being consistent and unified in setting boundaries for young people was seen as a team responsibility which could become a catalyst *"for a place to flourish"* *(INT 13)*. This educator understood being solid as being consistent with boundaries and how they are applied and having a common understanding around that as a member of a team. This was particularly important when team members had different perspectives and opinions about how certain issues should be handled. *"You need to participate as a whole team and I find that when one person doesn't participate, and it only takes one person, within this environment, the whole team has to carry it" (INT 13).*

Being spiritual and just

For staff working with young people in this context, being able to recognise the spiritual dimension of their work was seen as valuable. Being loving in an unconditional way and being able to recognise *"unconditional love" (INT 13)* as an essential aspect of the work, were expressions of spiritual dispositions that were valuable for developing relationships. Staff also equated being caring with expressions of being unconditionally loving and forgiving, commenting that *"All these kids realise is that no one gets expelled, what they're getting here is unconditional love and that constant forgiveness. They don't know that cause out in the world it's three strikes and you're gone" (INT 13).* In a similar vein another educator felt that everything functioned on the notion of unconditional love which she described as, *"a love for our work and a love for our young people and a love for what's going on . . . a love and respect for the circumstances that are going on* [in young people's lives]*" (INT 15).*

If staff were wanting to foster the disposition of being spiritual and just, they may seek to demonstrate the disposition of being able to encourage aspiration and values in others. For example, one adult educator encouraged young people *"to be a bigger person" (INT 5)* as an internalised state, especially when faced with challenges. Being just and being ethical was expressed when educators were being responsive to the needs of those who were marginalised, for example, those in physical or literal poverty. Other dispositions of spirituality and justice included being able to recognise social justice and the responsibility of solidarity and political action. Being socially inclusive and just, and being *"open to learn from young people and their families" (INT 16)* were also expressions of the disposition of being spiritual and just.

Intentionally Cultivating a Broader Range of Personal Dispositions

The personal dispositions evident in the interview data offer insights into ways of being that actively support authentic relational practice. These dispositions are useful to consider in critical self-reflection and reflective practice processes in teams. In particular, reflecting on personal dispositions that are a practitioner's strengths can be an affirming process. Additionally, consideration of how a broader range of personal dispositions can be cultivated is a worthwhile exercise for professional learning and growth. For example:

- *What personal dispositions might you, in your role as an educator, intentionally cultivate over a period of time?*
- *How might feedback from young people and colleagues guide you in your consideration of which personal dispositions to focus on to improve your relational practice?*
- *What support, mentoring and feedback options might be necessary for you, in order to do this significant inner work of cultivating a wider repertoire of personal dispositions?*

8

In conclusion: A spatial metaphor

The common aspects of relational practice synthesised from the findings of my research project were not intended as a singular representation of educator identity and development in practice nor of the definitive influences of the flexi schools context. The synthesis of common aspects of relational practice has created a way of contributing further details to the map of the territory of flexi schools and learning choices programs. The metaphor used by te Riele (2012) of a "map for the future" is relevant for my research and has been adopted here for the purpose of drawing conclusions. Some significant landmarks and other key features of the landscape of the practice of educators in flexi school contexts have been identified. These key features have included a range of influences on educator identity and development in practice from the context.

The spatial metaphor associated with map making may be useful in so far as it offers an insight similar to early historical attempts to map unfamiliar geographical regions or territories. Early attempts at mapping territories always involved the interpretation of the mapmakers. They were not aided by sophisticated technological instruments such as satellite navigation resulting in an exact representation in a map. In a similar way the exploration of educator identity and development in practice in flexi schools has occurred within a relatively new education sector and within a fairly recent field of research. The process of adding detail to the map of the territory of flexi schools, specifically about how the context influences educator identity and development in practice, was an initial exploratory attempt to add further detail to the map of the field for the future.

The nature of this study drawing on the stories and experiences of educator's reflecting on their practice, has primarily been a twofold process. First, the process of capturing and documenting the stories and perceptions of those who have navigated the journey of being and becoming educators in flexi schools enabled the voice of practitioners to be heard. Second, the research provided opportunities to add more detail to the map of the territory, about educator identity and development in practice. It may open up further opportunities for adding finer detail to the map in the future, and to include young people's perspectives.

List of Appendices

Appendix A
Literature Review Extract. Three research perspectives and key researchers identified in the literature review of alternative education and learning choices programs

Appendix B
Themed groups of features of best practice in alternative education summarised from the literature review

Appendix C
Relational dispositions with examples from practitioners

Appendix A

Three Research Perspectives and Key Researchers Identified in the Literature Review of Alternative Education and Learning Choices Programs

Research portraying young people's viewpoint and experiences	Research foregrounding program features, typologies and program evaluation	Research presenting a critical perspective: sociological, ideological, political and policy issues impacting young people
Key informants' experiences (Fraser et al., 1997; O'Brien et al., 2001; Smyth et al., 2004; Taylor, 2009; te Riele, 2000)	Typologies of alternative education and features of best practice (Aron, 2003; Aron, 2006; de Jong, 2005; de Jong & Griffiths, 2006; DEETYA, 2001; Gable et al., 2006; Lehr, Chee, & Ysseldyke, 2009; Powell, 2003; Quinn et al., 2006; Raywid, 1994; Reimer & Cash, 2003; Tobin & Sprague, 1999)	Challenging issues of transitions (te Riele, 2004; te Riele & Crump, 2003)
Needs of young people (Bond, 2010; Zweig, 2003)	Promoting preventative programs and alternative models of schooling (Axford & Little, 2006; Case & Haines, 2004; te Riele, 2009)	Marginalisation of young people (te Riele, 2006)

	Different views of the nature of education (Fielding & Moss, 2011; te Riele, 2009),	Sociological studies of young people (Wyn, 2008)	Indicators of disadvantage and social exclusion (Saunders, Naidoo, & Griffiths, 2007)	Contradictions of alternative education programs (de Jong, 2005; Vadeboncoeur, 2009) Critique of educational policy for young people (te Riele, 2011)
Impact of schooling on young people (Bond, 2011; Lumby & Morrison, 2009; Smyth, 2003; Smyth & Hattam, 2002; Smyth et al., 2004)	Describing sustainable programs (Cassidy & Bates, 2005; Cole, 2004; Tobin & Sprague, 2000),	Young people's perspectives on futures (Stokes, Wierenga, & Wyn, 2003) Comparisons between conventional education & other flexible learning options (Connor, 2006)	Relationship of young people with teachers in schools and staff in alternative education and learning choices programs (Croninger & Lee, 2001; Mills & McGregor, 2010; Quinn et al., 2006; Wilson et al., 2011) Scans of alternative education and flexible learning choices programs (de Jong, 2005; Holdsworth, 2011; Mills & McGregor, 2010; Powell & Shafiq, 2009; te Riele, 2012)	Evaluation of programs (Halsey, Jones, & Lord, 2006; Myconos, 2011; Reimer & Cash, 2003; Te Puni Kokiri, 2004; Walsh & Tilbury, 2011)

Appendix B

Themed Groups of Features of Best Practice in Alternative Education Summarised from the Literature Review

Education of the whole person	Young person-centred learning choices	Supportive and highly skilled multidisciplinary staff	Integration with quality community connections
An holistic approach to education catering to the young person's social, emotional, physical, spiritual and intellectual needs	A student-centred approach to learning	High quality staff including those from non-teaching backgrounds	Family/carer involvement
(de Jong, 2005; de Jong & Griffiths, 2006; Department of Employment, Education, Training and Youth Affairs (DEETYA), 2001; Lange & Sletten, 2002; Mills & McGregor, 2010; O'Brien, Thesing, & Herbert, 2001; Reimer & Cash, 2003; Tobin & Sprague, 2000)	(Aron, 2003; Cole, 2004; de Jong, 2005; de Jong & Griffiths, 2006; DEETYA, 2001; Lange & Sletten, 2002; Mills & McGregor, 2010; O'Brien et al., 2001; Tobin & Sprague, 1999, 2000; Walsh & Tilbury, 2011)	(Aron, 2003; Cole, 2004; de Jong & Griffiths, 2006; DEETYA, 2001; O'Brien et al., 2001; Tobin & Sprague, 1999; Walsh & Tilbury, 2011)	(Aron, 2003; Cole, 2004; de Jong, 2005; de Jong & Griffiths, 2006; DEETYA, 2001; O'Brien et al., 2001; Tobin & Sprague, 1999, 2000)

Theme	References
A safe and supportive learning environment	(Aron, 2003; 2006; de Jong, 2005; de Jong & Griffiths, 2006; Lange & Sletten, 2002; Mills & McGregor, 2010; O'Brien et al., 2001; Reimer & Cash, 2003; Tobin & Sprague, 2000)
Flexible delivery of curriculum	(Cole, 2004; de Jong, 2005; de Jong & Griffiths, 2006; Lange & Sletten, 2002; Mills & McGregor, 2010; O'Brien et al., 2001; Tobin & Sprague, 1999)
A strong emphasis on positive relationships rather than punitive behaviour management	(Aron, 2003; de Jong, 2005; de Jong & Griffiths, 2006; Mills & McGregor, 2010; O'Brien et al., 2001; Tobin & Sprague, 1999, 2000)
Presence of mentors	(de Jong, 2005; de Jong & Griffiths, 2006; Lange & Sletten, 2002; O'Brien et al., 2001; Tobin & Sprague, 1999, 2000)
Small class sizes	(Aron, 2003; 2006; de Jong, 2005; de Jong & Griffiths, 2006; Lange & Sletten, 2002; Mills & McGregor, 2010; O'Brien et al., 2001; Tobin & Sprague, 1999, 2000; Walsh & Tilbury, 2011)
Life-skills education	(Aron, 2003; de Jong & Griffiths, 2006; Mills & McGregor, 2010; Tobin & Sprague, 1999, 2000)
Proactive rather than reactive responses to young people	(de Jong, 2005; de Jong & Griffiths, 2006; Mills & McGregor, 2010; O'Brien et al., 2001)
Interagency collaboration	(Aron, 2006; Cole, 2004; de Jong, 2005; de Jong & Griffiths, 2006; DEETYA, 2001; Mills & McGregor, 2010; Tobin & Sprague, 2000)

Transition to employment	Encouragement of active participation and responsibility of young people for their learning	Community linkages
(Aron, 2003; 2006; de Jong, 2005; de Jong & Griffiths, 2006; DEETYA, 2001; Lange & Sletten, 2002; O'Brien et al., 2001)	(Aron, 2003; Cole, 2004; de Jong, 2005; de Jong & Griffiths, 2006; Mills & McGregor, 2010; O'Brien et al., 2001)	(Aron, 2003; 2006; Cole, 2004; de Jong, 2005; de Jong & Griffiths, 2006; DEETYA, 2001; Mills & McGregor, 2010; O'Brien et al., 2001; Tobin & Sprague, 2000; Walsh & Tilbury, 2011)

Appendix C

Relational Dispositions with Examples from Practitioners

Dispositions of Relationships	Specific examples from practitioners' responses
Relationships Dispositions of embodying the principles (respect, participation, safe and legal, & honesty)	• Being able to embody the principles • Being able to authentically embody the principles • Being able to enact and embody the principles • Being able to embrace the principles in whole of life • Being able to embody the principles as a unified staff team • Being participatory in a unified staff • Being able to apply the four principles to self and others • Being authentic and consistent in living the principles • Being consistent in applying the principles to own behaviour and attitudes • Being able to engage with the principles at personal and professional levels e.g., being loving and authentic • Being able to embody the principles to encourage honesty, trust, safety and participation from others to have a go and take a risk • Being able to role-model in accordance with the principles • Being able to self-reflect and internalise the principles • Being able to recognise democracy and equity in the principles • Being able to resolve conflict non-violently using the principles

Dispositions of respect	• Being respectful • Being respectful and gentle • Being respectful and able to recognise/ encourage other's strength • Being respectful of the circumstances in young people's lives • Being respected
Dispositions of safety	• Being able to recognise the many dimensions of safety (emotional, spiritual, physical & intellectual) • Being able to recognise safety as a basic human need • Being safe to express yourself
Dispositions of honesty	• Being honest • Being honest with self about not knowing everything
Dispositions of being relational	• Being able to recognise primary importance of relationships • Being able to see curriculum as secondary to relationships • Being able to recognise the difficulties of relationships for young people • Being willing to build genuine relationships • Being patient, accepting and understanding in relationships • Being challenging and compassionate in genuine relationship with young people • Being able to engage/ maintain genuine relationship • Being relational by being available and accessible • Being able to establish and maintain genuine connection • Being present to others and genuinely interested in their wellbeing

Dispositions of openness	• Being open
	• Being open and honest
	• Being open to admit mistakes
	• Being able to learn from mistakes
	• Being willing to make amends
	• Being able to recognise storytelling as opening up to others
	• Being able to listen to young people and what they're looking for
	• Being open in mind and attitude
	• Being open and willing to seek assistance
	• Being open/honest and vulnerable in relationships with young people
	• Being open and honest about feelings
	• Being able to discuss emotional upsets
	• Being open about caring for others
	• Being open, approachable and trustworthy
	• Being open in relationships
	• Being available and open to learn from listening
Dispositions of commitment	• Being committed
	• Being committed to young people's needs
	• Being committed to the young people
	• Being able to recognise personal responsibility
	• Being able to recognise collective/ collaborative approach to responsibility
	• Being accountable to the school community
	• Being able to recognise the importance of commitment and support in ongoing relationships

Dispositions of generosity	• Being able to appreciate generosity in all • Being able to appreciate generosity in its different forms
Dispositions of caring and compassion	• Being caring • Being firm and caring • Being compassionate
Dispositions of hospitality	• Being hospitable • Being welcoming • Being able to encourage participation by welcoming others • Being non-judgemental
Dispositions of role modelling	• Being a role model • Being a role model and mentor • Being able to recognise influence of self on others and others on self, including young people • Being a co-learner • Being able to learn through participation in doing and being • Being sensitive to others • Being able to recognise strength in others • Being able to recognise the development of capacity in others

Dispositions of support	• Being supportive
	• Being supportive of the growth and development of others to be happy with themselves
	• Being supportive and able to work alongside others
	• Being supportive through expressing generosity, care and respect
	• Being able to recognise the confidence level in others and support the development of this to enable positive risk taking
	• Being able to value the support of others
	• Being supported by others
	• Being part of a unified staff team
	• Being able to recognise tendency of young people to mask difficulties
Dispositions of authenticity	• Being authentic
	• Being able to recognise the heart – not ruled by the head
	• Being authentic in relationships
	• Being able to be yourself
	• Being able to recognise self-value and strengths
	• Being able to appreciate the importance of humour
	• Being able to recognise the humanity of every young person
	• Being able to recognise the balance between: o Teaching and learning o Development of decency in each person
	• Being playful/ young at heart
	• Being human

Dispositions of understanding and patience	• Being understanding at a deep level • Being understanding and willing to take time with others • Being trusting and demonstrating trust in an ongoing way • Being patient • Being patient and able to develop this • Being patient in supporting staff • Being patient and tolerant
Dispositions of consistency	• Being consistent • Being consistent and unified in setting boundaries
Dispositions of spirituality and justice	• Being able to recognise the spiritual dimension of the work • Being loving • Being unconditionally loving • Being able to recognise 'unconditional love' as an essential aspect of the work • Being forgiving • Being just • Being ethical • Being able to recognise social justice and responsibility of solidarity and political action • Being responsive to the needs of those that are marginalised (e.g., those in physical/literal poverty) • Being socially inclusive and just and open to learn from young people and their families • Being able to encourage aspiration and values in other

References

Ageyev, V. (2003). Vygotsky in the mirror of cultural interpretations. In A. Kozulin, B. Gindis, V. Ageyev, & S. M. Miller (Eds.), *Vygotsky's educational theory in cultural context* (pp. 432-450). Cambridge: Cambridge University Press.

Alpert, B. (1991). Students' resistance in the classroom. *Anthropology & Education Quarterly, 22*(4), 350-366. doi: 10.2307/3195659

Alsup, J. (2006). *Teacher identity discourses: Negotiating personal and professional spaces.* Mahwah, NJ: Lawrence Erlbaum

Apple, M. W., & Beane, J. A. (2007). Schooling for democracy. *Principal Leadership*, 8(2), 34--38.

Aron, L. Y. (2003). *Towards a typology of alternative education programs: A compilation of elements from the literature.* Washington D.C.: Urban Institute.

Aron, L. Y. (2006). *An overview of alternative education.* Washington D.C.: The Urban Institute.

Axford, N., & Little, M. (2006). Refocusing children's services towards prevention: Lessons from the literature. *Children and Society 20*, 299-312. doi: 10.1002/CHI.894

Ayers, W. (2009). Teaching in and for democracy. *Kappa Delta Pi Record*, 46(1), 30-33.

Bakhtin, M. M. (1981). *The dialogic imagination* (C. Emerson & M. Holquist, Trans.). Austin, Texas: University of Texas Press.

Beck, K., & Cassidy, W. (2009). Embeddwing the ethic of care in school policies and practices. In K. Te Riele (Ed.), *Making schools different: Alternative approaches to educating young people* (pp.55-64). London: Sage Publications.

Beijaard, D. (1995). Teachers' prior experiences and actual perceptions of professional identity. *Teachers and Teaching: Theory and Practice, 1*(2), 281-294. doi: 10.1080/1354060950010209

Berry, T. (2006). *The dream of the earth*. San Francisco: Sierra Club Books.

Biesta, G. (2004). "Mind the Gap!" Communication and the educational relation. In C. Bingham & A. M. Sidorkin (Eds.), *No education without Relation*. New York: Peter Lang.

Bingham, C. (2004). Let's treat authority relationally. In C. Bingham & A. M. Sidorkin (Eds.), *No education without relation* (pp. 23-37). New York: Peter Lang.

Boaler, J. (2008). Promoting 'relational equity' and high mathematics achievement through an innovative mixed-ability approach. *British Educational Research Journal, 34*(2), 167-194. doi: 10.1080/01411920701532145

Bond, S. (2010). *Integrated service delivery for young people: A literature review*. Fitzroy, VIC: Brotherhood of St Laurence.

Bond, S. (2011). *Overcoming barriers to education: Peninsula youth connections evaluation, Stage 1 Report*. Fitzroy, VIC: Brotherhood of St Laurence.

Britzman, D., P. (2003). *Practice makes practice: A critical study of learning to teach* (Revised ed.). New York: State University of New York Press.

Capra, F. (1975). *The Tao of physics: An exploration of the parallels between modern physics and Eastern mysticism*. Berkeley, CA: Shambhala Publications.

Capra, F. (1997). *The web of life*. New York: Knopf Doubleday Publishing Group.

Capra, F. (2004). *The hidden connections: A science for sustainable living*. New York: Knopf Doubleday Publishing Group.

Case, S., & Haines, K. (2004). Promoting prevention: Evaluating a multi-agency initiative of youth consultation and crime prevention in Swansea. *Children and Society, 18*, 355 - 370. doi: 10.1002/CHI.814

Cassidy, W., & Bates, A. (2005). "Drop-outs" and "Push-outs": Finding hope at a school that actualizes the ethic of care. *American Journal of Education, 112*(1), 66-102. doi: 10.1086/444524

Cassidy, W., & Chinnery, A. (2009). Learning from Indigenous education. In K. Te Riele (Ed.), *Making schools different: Alternative approaches to educating young people* (pp.135-143). London: Sage.

Cole, P. (2004). Learning in alternative settings: What makes a sustainable program? Retrieved from http://dusseldorp.org.au/wp-content/uploads/2014/lc/docs/Learning_Settings.pdf

Cole, M. (2009). The perils of translation: A first step in reconsidering Vygotsky's Theory of Development in relation to formal education. *Mind, Culture, and Activity, 16*(4), 291-295. doi: 10.1080/10749030902795568

Connor, J. (2006). *What's mainstream? Conventional and unconventional learning in Logan.* Retrieved from http://www.voced.edu.au/content/ngv:34138

Covey, S. (2011). *The 3rd alternative: Solving life's most difficult problems.* London: Simon & Schuster.

Croninger, R., & Lee, V. (2001). Social capital and dropping out of high school: Benefits to at-risk students of teachers' support and guidance. *Teachers College Record, 103*(4), 548-581.

de Chardin, P. T. (1959). *The phenomenon of man.* Retrieved from http://archive.org/details/phenomenon-of-man-pierre-teilhard-de-chardin.pdf

de Jong, T. (2005). A framework of principles and best practice for managing student behaviour in the Australian education context. *School Psychology International, 26*, 353-370. doi: 10.1177/0143034305055979

de Jong, T., & Griffiths, C. (2006). The role of alternative education programs in meeting the needs of adolescent students with challenging behaviour: Characteristics of best practice. *Australian Journal of Guidance and Counselling, 16*(1).

Delors, J. (1999). Education: The treasure within. *Education Quarterly Review, 6*(1), 10-19.

Department of Education, Employment, Training and Youth Affairs (DEETYA). (2001). *Doing it well: Case studies of innovation and best practice in working with at risk young people.* Canberra: DEETYA.

Dewey, J. (2010). *Democracy and Education: An Introduction to the Philosophy of Education* (Revised ed.). Los Angeles, CA: Indo European Publishing.

Diez, M. E. (2007). Looking back and moving forward: Three tensions in the teacher dispositions discourse *Journal of Teacher Education 58*(5), 388-396. doi: 10.1177/0022487107308418

Downey, L. (2009). *From isolation to connection: A guide to understanding and working with traumatised children and young people.* Melbourne, Victoria: Child Safety Commissioner.

Dweck, C. (2006). *Mindset: The new psychology of success.* New York: Random House

Dwyer, P., & Wyn, J. (2001). *Youth, education and risk: Facing the future.* London: Routledge Falmer.

Edwards, A. (2005). Relational agency: Learning to be a resourceful practitioner. *International Journal of Educational Research, 43,* 168-182. doi: 10.1016/j.ijer.2006.06.010

Edwards, A. (2004). The New Multi-Agency Working: Collaborating to Prevent the Social Exclusion of Children and Families. *Journal of Integrated Care, 12*(5), 3-9.

Fielding, M., & Moss, P. (2011). *Radical education and the common school.* Oxford: Routledge.

Flippin, Jr., W. E. (2012, Month, date). Ubuntu: Applying African philosophy in building community [Blog post]. Huffington Post Blog. Retrieved from https://www.huffingtonpost.com/reverend-william-e-flippin-jr/ubuntu-applying-african-p_b_1243904.html

Fook, J., & Gardner, F. (2007). *Practising critical reflection: A resource handbook.* Maidenhead, UK: Open University Press.

Foundation for Young Australians (FYA). (2017). The New Work Mindset. *New Work Order Series.* Sydney: Alphabeta.

Fraser, J., Davis, P., & Singh, R. (1997). Identity work by alternative high school students. *International Journal of Qualitative Studies in Education, 10*(2), 221-235. doi: 10.1080/095183997237313

Freire, P. (2000). *Pedagogy of the Oppressed* (M. Bergman Ramos, Trans. 30th Anniversary ed.). New York: Continuum.

Friesen, D. W., Finney, S., & Krentz, C. (1999). Together against all odds: towards understanding the identities of teachers of at risk students. *Teaching and Teacher Education, 15*(8), 923-932. doi: 10.1016/s0742-051x(99)00035-9

Gable, R. A., Bullock, L. M., & Evans, W. H. (2006). Changing perspectives on alternative schooling for children and adolescents with challenging behavior. *Preventing School Failure: Alternative Education for Children and Youth, 51*(1), 5-9. doi: 10.3200/PSFL.51.1.5-9

Gair, S., Miles, D., & Thomson, J. (2005). Reconciling Indigenous and Non-Indigenous knowledges in social work education: Action and legitimacy. *Journal of Social Work Education* 41(2), 179-190.

Gergen, K. J. (2009). *Relational being: Beyond self and community.* Oxford: Oxford University Press.

Halsey, K., Jones, M., & Lord, P. (2006). What Works in Stimulating Creativity Amongst Socially Excluded Young People. Berkshire, UK: National Foundation for Educational Research

Holdsworth, R. (2011). Learning Choices National Scan: Programs and schools catering for young people at risk of not completing their education. Melbourne: Dusseldorp Skills Forum.

Holman, P. (2010). *Engaging emergence: Turning upheaval into opportunity.* San Francisco, CA: Berrett-Koehhler.

Holman, P., Devane, T., Cady, S., & Associates. (2007). *The change handbook: the definitive resource on today's best methods for engaging whole systems* Retrieved from http://peggyholman.com/wp-content/uploads/2010/06/From-Chaos-to-Coherence.pdf

Horn, M. (2010). Enabling participation: Integrated services for disadvantaged job seekers. Brotherhood Comment August, pp.1-2. Retrieved from http://library.bsl.org.au/jspui/bitstream/1/6896/1/BSL_Brotherhood_Comment_Aug2010.pdf

Hutchby, I. (2005). "Active Listening": Formulations and the elicitation of feelings-talk in child counselling. *Research on Language & Social Interaction, 38*(3), 303-329. doi: 10.1207/s15327973rlsi3803_4

Jeffs, T., & Smith, M. K. (2005). *Informal education: Conversation, democracy and learning* (3rd Revised ed.). Nottingham: Educational Heretics Press.

Kalantzis, M., & Cope, B. (2005). *Learning by design.* Melbourne: Common Ground Publishing.

Knudston, P., & Suzuki, D. (1992). *Wisdom of the elders.* North Sydney, NSW: Allen and Unwin.

Lange, C. M., & Sletten, S. J. (2002). *Alternative education: A brief history and research synthesis.* Alexandria, VA.: National Association of State Directors of Special Education

Lederach, J. P. (2005). *The moral imagination: The art and soul of building peace.* New York: Oxford University Press.

Lehr, C. A., Chee, S. T., & Ysseldyke, J. (2009). Alternative schools: A synthesis of State-level policy and research. *Remedial and Special Education, 30*(19), 19-32. doi: 10.1177/0741932508315645

Lumby, J., & Morrison, M. (2009). Youth perspectives: schooling, capabilities frameworks and human rights. *International Journal of Inclusive Education, 13*(6), 581-596. doi: 10.1080/13603110801995920

Macy, J. (1991). *World as lover, world as self.* Berkeley, CA: Parallax Press.

Macy, J., & Johnstone, C. (2012). *Active hope: How to face the mess we're in without going crazy.* Novato, CA: New World Library.

Margonis, F. (2004). From student resistance to educative engagement: A case study in building powerful student-teacher relationships. In C. Bingham & A. M. Sidorkin (Eds.), *No education without relation.* New York: Peter Lang.

Matthews, C., Watego, L., Cooper, T., & Baturo, A. (2005). *Does mathematics education in Australia devalue Indigenous culture? Indigenous perspectives and non-Indigenous reflections.* Paper presented at the 28th conference of the Mathematics Education Research Group of Australasia, Melbourne, VIC.

McCashen, W. (2005). *The strengths approach.* Bendigo: Innovative Resources.

Miller, T. (2005). Across the great divide: Creating partnerships in education. In R. Carnwell & J. Buchanan (Eds.), *Effective practice in health and social care: A partnership approach.* Buckingham: Open University Press.

Mills, M., & McGregor, G. (2010). *Re-engaging Students in Education: Success Factors in Alternative Schools.* Brisbane: Youth Affairs Network Queensland Inc.

Ministerial Council on Education, Employment, Training and Youth Affairs (MCEETYA). (2008). *Melbourne declaration on the educational goals for young Australians.* Melbourne: Curriculum Corporation. Retrieved from http://www.curriculum.edu.au/verve/_resources/National_Declaration_on_the_Educational_Goals_for_Young_Australians.pdf

Morgan, A. (2013). *Different ways of being an educator: A sociocultural exploration of educator identity and development in practice, in a system of non-traditional flexi schools* (Unpublished PhD thesis). Griffith University. Brisbane, Australia.

Morgan, A. (2016). Cultivating critical reflection: Educators making sense and meaning of professional identity and relational dynamics in complex practice. *Teaching Education, 28*(1), 41-55.

Morgan, A., Brown, R., Heck, D., Pendergast, D., & Kanasa, H. (2013). Professional identity pathways of educators in alternative schools: The utility of reflective practice groups for educator induction and professional learning. *Reflective Practice, 14,* (2), 258-270. doi: 10.1080/14623943.2012.749227

Morgan, A., Pendergast, D., Brown, R., & Heck, D. (2014). The art of holding complexity: a contextual influence on educator identity and development in practice in a system of alternative 'flexi' schools. *Reflective Practice, 15*(5), 579-591. doi: 10.1080/14623943.2014.900020

Morgan, A., Pendergast, D., Brown, R., & Heck, D. (2015). Relational ways of being an educator: Trauma-informed practice supporting disenfranchised young people. *International Journal of Inclusive Education, 19*(10), 1037-1051.

Myconos, G. (2011). *A path to re-engagement. Evaluating the first year of a Community VCAL education program for young people.* Fitzroy, Victoria: Brotherhood of St Laurence.

Nabavi, M., & Lund, D. (2010). Youth and social justice: A conversation on collaborative activism. In W. Linds, L. Goulet & A. Sammel (Eds.), *Emancipatory practices: Adult/youth engagement for social and environmental justice* (pp. 3-14). Rotterdam: Sense Publishers.

Noddings, N. (1992). The challenge to care in schools: An alternative approach to education (Vol. 8). New York: Teachers College Press.

O'Brien, P., Thesing, A., & Herbert, P. (2001). *Alternative education: Literature review and report on key informants' experiences.* Auckland, NZ: Ministry of Education.

Owen, H. (2008). *Wave Rider: Leadership for High Performance in a Self-Organizing World.* San Francisco: Berrett-Koehler.

Panofsky, C. P. (2003). The relations of learning and student social class: Toward Re-"socializing" sociocultural learning theory. In A. Kozulin, B. Gindis, V. Ageyev & S. M. Miller (Eds.), *Vygotsky's educational theory in cultural context.* Cambridge: Cambridge University Press.

Perry, B. D. (2009). Examining child maltreatment through a neurodevelopmental lens: Clinical applications of the neurosequential model of therapeutics. *Journal of Loss and Trauma: International Perspectives on Stress & Coping, 14*(4), 240-255. doi: 10.1080/15325020903004350

Powell, D., & Shafiq, T. (2009). *A snapshot of Queensland's "Re-Engagement" services.* Brisbane: YANQ.

Powell, D. E. (2003). Demystifying alternative education: Considering what really works *Reclaiming Children and Youth, 12*(2), 68-70.

Quinn, M. M., Poirier, J. M., Faller, S. E., Gable, R. A., & Tonelson, S. W. (2006). An examination of school climate in effective alternative programs. *Preventing School Failure: Alternative Education for Children and Youth, 51*(1), 11-17. doi: 10.3200/PSFL.51.1.11-17

Ratner, C. (2000). Outline of a coherent, comprehensive concept of culture. *Cross-Cultural Psychology Bulletin, 34*(1-2), 5-11.

Raywid, M. A. (1994). Alternative schools: The state of the art. *Educational Leadership, 52*(1), 26-31.

Reimer, M. S., & Cash, T. (2003). *Alternative schools: Best practice for development and evaluation.* Retrieved from http://eric.ed.gov/PDFS/ED481475.pdf

Renshaw, P. (2004). Dialogic learning, teaching and instruction: Theoretical roots and analytical frameworks. In J. van der Linden & P. Renshaw (Eds.), *Dialogic learning: Shifting perspectives to learning, instruction, and teaching* (pp. 1-15). Dordrecht: Kluwer Academic Press.

Rogers, C. R., & Farson, R. E. (1957). *Active listening.* Chicago: Industrial Relations Center, The University of Chicago.

Rueda, R., & Monzo, L. D. (2002). Apprenticeship for teaching: Professional development issues surrounding the collaborative relationship between teachers and paraeducators. *Teaching and Teacher Education 18,* 503-521.

Saunders, P., Naidoo, Y., & Griffiths, M. (2007). *Towards new indicators of disadvantage: Deprivation and social exclusion in Australia.* Sydney: Social Policy Research Centre

Scharmer, O. (2008). *Theory U: Leading from the future as it emerges.* San Francisco: Berrett-Koehler.

Senge, P. (2006). *The Fifth Discipline: The Art and Practice of the Learning Organization* (2nd ed.). London: Random House.

Senge, P., Scharmer, O., Jaworski, J., & Flowers, B. S. (2004). *Presence: Exploring profound change in people, organizations and society.* New York: Doubleday.

Sheehan, N., & Walker, P. (2001). The Purga Project: Indigenous knowledge research. *The Australian Journal of Indigenous Education, 29*(2), 11-17.

Sidorkin, A. M. (2000). Toward a pedagogy of relation. (Faculty Publications, Paper 17). Retrieved from http://digitalcommons.ric.edu/facultypublications/17

Siegel, D. J. (2006). An interpersonal neurobiology approach to psychotherapy. *Psychiatric Annals, 36*(4), 248-248-256.

Slattery, L., Butigan, K., Pelicaric, V., & Preston-Pile, K. (2005). *Engage: Exploring nonviolent living.* Oakland, CA: Pace e Bene Nonviolence Service.

Smith, M. (2008). What is pedagogy? Retrieved from http://www.infed.org/whatis/what_is_pedagogy.html

Smith, M. (2001). Young people, informal education and association. Retrieved from http://www.curriculum.edu.au/verve/_resources/National_Declaration_on_the_Educational_Goals_for_Young_Australians.pdf

Smyth, J. (2003). The making of young lives with/against the school credential. *Journal of Education and Work, 16*(2), 127-146.

Smyth, J. (2006). When students have 'relational' power: the school as a site for identity formation around engagement and school retention. Paper presented at the Australian Association for Research in Education, Adelaide.

Smyth, J., & Hattam, R. (2002). Early school leaving and the cultural geography of high schools. *British Educational Research Journal, 28*(3), 375-397.

Smyth, J., Hattam, R., with Cannon, J., Edwards, J., Wilson, N., & Wurst, S. (2004). *'Dropping out', drifting off, being excluded: Becoming somebody withoutsSchool.* New York: Peter Lang Publishing.

Starhawk. (1988). *Truth or dare: Encounters with power, authority and mystery.* San Francisco: Harper San Francisco.

Stokes, H., Wierenga, A., & Wyn, J. (2003). *Preparing for the future and living now: Young people's perceptions of Career Education, VET, Enterprise Education and part-time work.* Melbourne: Youth Research Centre.

Suzuki, D., with McConnell, A., & Mason, A. (2007). *The sacred balance: Rediscovering our place in nature, updated and expanded* (3rd ed.). Vancouver: Greystone Books.

Taylor, J. (2009). *Stories of early school leaving: Pointers for policy and practice.* Fitzroy: Brotherhood of St Laurence.

Te Puni Kokiri. (2004). *Alternative education: Effectiveness audit.* Wellington, NZ: State Sector Performance, Ministry of Maori Development

te Riele, K. (2000). *The best thing I've ever done: Second chance education for early school leavers.* Paper presented at the AARE, University of Sydney.

te Riele, K. (2004). Youth transition in Australia: Challenging assumptions of linearity and choice. *Journal of Youth Studies, 7*(3), 243-257. doi: 10.1080/1367626042000268908

te Riele, K. (2006). Youth 'at risk': Further marginalizing the marginalized? *Journal of Education Policy, 21*(2), 129-146. doi: 10.1080/02680930500499968

te Riele, K. (2007). Educational alternatives for marginalised youth. *Australian Educational Researcher, 34*(3), 53-68.

te Riele, K. (Ed.). (2009). *Making Schools Different: Alternative Approaches to Educating Young People.* London: Sage.

te Riele, K. (2011). Raising educational attainment: How young people's experiences speak back to the 'Compact with young Australians'. *Critical Studies in Education, 52*(1), 1-15. doi: 10.1080/17508487.2011.536515

te Riele, K. (2012). *Learning choices: A map for the future. Report to Dusseldorp Skills Forum.* Melbourne: Victoria Institute for Education, Diversity and Lifelong Learning.

te Riele, K., & Crump, S. (2003). Ongoing inequality in a 'knowledge economy': Perceptions and actions. *International Studies in Sociology of Education, 13*(1), 55-75. doi: 10.1080/09620210300200103

Thayer-Bacon, B. J. (2004). Personal and social relations. In C. Bingham & A. M. Sidorkin (Eds.), *No education without relation* (pp. 165-179). New York: Peter Lang.

Thompson, M. S., Entwisle, D. R., Alexander, K. L., & Sundius, M. J. (1992). The influence of family composition on children's conformity to the student role. *American Educational Research Journal, 29*(2), 405-424. doi: 10.2307/1163374

Tobin, T., & Sprague, J. (1999). Alternative education programs for at-risk youth: Issues, best practice, and recommendations. *Oregon School Study Council Bulletin, 42*(4), 1-19.

Tobin, T., & Sprague, J. (2000). Alternative education strategies: Reducing violence in school and the community. *Journal of Emotional and Behavioural Disorders, 8*(3), 177-186. doi: 10.1177/106342660000800305

UNESCO. (1994). *The Salamanca statement and framework for action on special needs education.* Salamanca, Spain.

Vadeboncoeur, J. A. (2009). Spaces of difference: The contradictions of alternative educational programs. *Educational Studies 45*(3), 280-299. doi: 10.1080/00131940902910974

Vadeboncoeur, J. A. (2011). Youth engagement in educational contexts. Youth+ Whole Staff Days. Video conference lecture University of Queensland, Brisbane.

Vadeboncoeur, J. A. (2012). *Place making with youth: A process for mediating resilience.* Youth+ Whole Staff Days. Videoconference lecture. University of Queensland, Brisbane.

Vadeboncoeur, J. A. & Vellos, R. E., (2016). Re-creating social futures: The role of the moral imagination in student-teacher relationships in alternative education. *International Journal of Child, Youth and Family Studies, 7,* 307-323. doi: 10.18357/ijcyfs72201615723

Vygotsky, L. (1978). *Mind in society: The development of higher psychological processes.* Cambridge, MA: Harvard University Press.

Walsh, P., & Tilbury, C. (2011). *Bridge Program Evaluation Report: A report to Edmund Rice Education Australia Youth+ on the evaluation of the Bridge Program.* Brisbane: Griffith University.

Warren, M. (2005). Communities and schools: A new view of urban education reform. *Harvard Educational Review 75*(2).

West, L. (2010). Really reflexive practice: Auto/biographical research and struggles for a critical reflexivity. In H. Bradbury, N. Frost, S. Kilminster & M. Zukas (Eds.), *Beyond reflective practice: New approaches to professional lifelong learning* (pp. 66-80). London: Routledge.

Wheatley, M., J. (2006). *Leadership and the New Science: Discovering order in a chaotic world* (3rd ed.). San Francisco: Berrett-Koehler.

Whitby, G. (2013). *Educating Gen Wi-Fi: How to make schools relevant for 21st Century learners.* Sydney: Harper Collins.

Wilson, K., Stemp, K., & McGinty, S. (2011). Re-engaging young people with education and training: What are the alternatives?. *Youth Studies Australia, 30*(4), 32-39.

Wyn, J. (2008). *The changing context of Australian youth and its implications for social inclusion*. Paper presented at the Social Inclusion and Youth Workshop Melbourne. http://www.bsl.org.au/main.asp?PageId=6175

Youth Sector Training Manual. (1990) (3rd edition). Brisbane: Division of Youth, Department of Tourism, Sport and Racing. Qld.

Zweig, J. (2003). *Vulnerable youth: Identifying their need for alternative educational settings*. Washington D.C: The Urban Institute.